D1032568

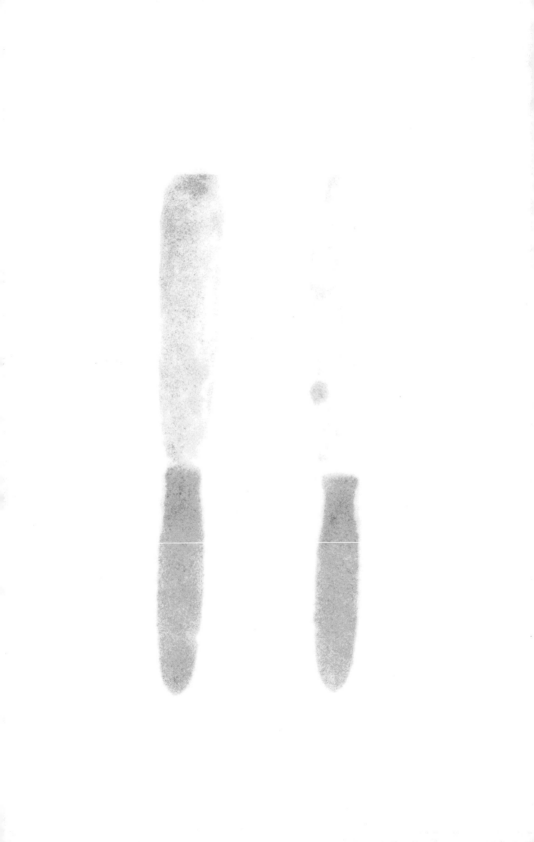

New York University School of Law
Series in Legal History
Board of Editors

Linden Studies in Legal History

The Linden studies in legal history, honoring Bella L. Linden, have been established by New York University School of Law, in appreciation of her contributions to the School, and by her friends, in recognition of her distinguished service at the New York bar.

New York University School of Law
Series in Legal History: 2

Murdering Mothers:
Infanticide in England
and New England
1558 - 1803

Peter C. Hoffer
and
N. E. H. Hull

Linden Studies in Anglo-American Legal History

New York University Press · New York and London
1981

Library of Congress Cataloging in Publication Data

Hoffer, Peter C.
  Murdering mothers.

  (New York University School of Law
Series in Legal history)
  Includes bibliographical references and index.
    1. Infanticide—England—History. 2. Infanti-
cide—New England—History. I. Hull, N. E. H.,
1949–   . II. Title. III. Series.
HV6541.G72E54   364.1'523   81-1235
ISBN 0-8147-3412-X   AACR2

For our parents:
Louis and Ruth Hoffer
Irene and William Hull

Contents

Introduction

In England and America, infanticide has been a crime that will not die. It first appeared in premodern times, arising from the struggle for survival against overpopulation and want, but it has persisted in the midst of postindustrial plenty. It is a crime rooted in indifference for infants, which survives in a modern "child-centered" culture. If the act made economic sense to the isolated, medieval villagers who practiced it, to modern English and American observers it is a shocking tragedy.

The subject of this book is the emergence of the modern law on infanticide in England and New England. Between 1558 and 1803, the law concerning infanticide and the treatment of suspects in the criminal justice systems of England and New England attained their present form. Premodern English authorities condemned the act of child murder, but they did not energetically suppress it. Few cases of infanticide were tried in the king's courts. As cases of the crime seemed to multiply in late Tudor and early Stuart England and her colonies, angered magistrates and troubled lawmakers reacted decisively. Between 1558 and 1700, early modern lawmakers and judges made the first

concerted effort to put an end to infanticide. Harsh court
rulings on motive and culpability were soon followed by the
severe statute of 1624, rendering the concealment of the
death of a newborn bastard presumptive evidence of murder. Over the course of the next century, this severity
turned into leniency. To learn how this transformation occurred, we have compared trials for infanticide in sixteenth-
and seventeenth-century courts with eighteenth-century
prosecutions. We have traced common law and statutory
pronouncements on the crime from notes in early Tudor
manuals for justices of the peace to essays on the reform of
capital punishment at the beginning of the nineteenth century. We have observed the way in which changing sexual
mores and ideas of maternal sentiment affected judges and
juries in the courtroom, leading ultimately to very low conviction rates and minimal sentences.

The rise and fall in frequency of infanticide cases in the
criminal records of these years is striking. Before Elizabeth
I ascended the throne, few cases appeared in the court files.
Late Tudor and early Stuart criminal tribunals, in contrast,
witnessed a leap in indictments and a still steeper climb in
the percentage of guilty verdicts. Prosecution and conviction rates continued high until the first decades of the eighteenth century, when they began a sharp and steady decline.
New England courts of "life and limb" encountered the
same rise and fall in cases and guilty verdicts.

Behind the accusations and trials we have discovered a
combination of legal, social, economic, and cultural influences. Elizabethan and Jacobean justices and lawmakers, tu-
tored by religious doctrine and confronted by the breakdown of traditional society, came to focus upon the crime
of infanticide. Their enmity for immoral women contributed to a wave of indictments for this offense. At the same
time, the very social and economic dislocations which disturbed the authorities were pressuring young unmarried
women to rid themselves of unwanted children. In the next
century, growing toleration for illicit sexuality and improving material conditions joined with the rise of romantic sen-

timentality to alter the views of judges and jurors, with modifications of the law of infanticide soon following.

These changes must be seen from two perspectives to be fully understood: that of the administrators of the law and that of the defendants. This book is therefore divided into two parts. Part I of the book views the prosecution of infanticide in the courts as an episode in the administration of criminal justice. The intrusion of parliament and the king's courts into the area of sexual morality, the rise of Puritanism, and the emergence of a landless laboring class begin this story. Examination of the transmission of English precedent and English morals to Puritan New England permits further exploration of the maturation of early modern infanticide law. Finally, comprehensive study of eighteenth-century cases, commentary, and statutes reveals the roots of modern leniency in verdicts and sentencing.

Part II portrays the criminal law from the perspective of the defendant. Criminal behavior, and the effort to punish it, are part of the social life of a community. Study of the characteristics of the accused and the external "environmental" causes of infanticide captures the relationship between law enforcement and social realities. The three chapters of Part II combine statistical analysis of the criminal record with forays into popular literature and borrowings from the sociology of crime and forensic psychiatry. Chapter 4 uncovers the features of the typical offender and ties these to her experience in the dock. Chapter 5 explains changes in multiple-year totals of infanticide as a function of environmental forces—the external causes of the crime. Economic needs, sexual norms, medical and demographic events, and levels of stress and violence in the society as a whole all had measurable affects upon the frequency of infanticide prosecutions—enabling us to calculate the composite effects of external conditions upon the amount of infanticide tried in the courts. The sixth chapter probes the inner motivation of individual offenders, employing concepts from clinical and social psychology, and ranging over subjects from abortion to sociopathology.

The Epilogue traces the occurrence and treatment of in-fanticide in England and America from the end of our nar-rative to the present. Its message is simple: Despite the mit-igation of the law, many of the underlying emotional causes of infanticide we have found in early modern Anglo-Amer-ican society persist today. Reform of the law has not been an answer to this problem.

Five appendices conclude this book. The first four are quantitative essays of varying complexity designed to give additional insights into topics discussed in the body of the book. In addition, each of these statistical exercises is rele-vant to further inquiry into the history of law enforcement. The last appendix provides a summary of the data used to study the causes of death in eighteenth-century London and its environs.

Definitions, Sources, and Methods

It is not an easy task for legal historians to define infanticide, for "infancy" has a great variety of legal meanings. English and American early modern criminal law did not use the term "infanticide." In law, premeditated killing of a newborn or an older child was a murder. We did not wish to limit ourselves to neonaticide—the killing of a newborn within its first day of life—lest we overlook potentially large numbers of older victims. Our upper age limit had to include cases of older child murder, while not blurring the distinction between dependent young children, the victims we sought to trace, and economically viable adolescents. To retain our focus, we elected to adhere to but one of the many legal definitions of "infant" given in early modern English criminal law. In Tudor homicide trials, an "infant," a child under the "age of discretion," was defined to be eight years old or younger. The "infant" could not be prosecuted for the capital crime, nor sworn to give evidence (3 Henry VII, c. 1). This was a definition clear to magistrates and judges. The "age of discretion" given in manuals like Dalton's *The Countrey Justice* (1619), read and used in both England and New England, was nine years old.

This definition is broad enough to include a wide variety of child murders. While the bulk of our cases are parental neonaticides, we have included in our totals the murder of all children under the age of nine, by strangers as well as relatives. We have included indictments for murder by exposure, starvation, neglect, and long-term abuse, as well as violent assault. Our aim was consistency; if the victim was an "infant" and the defendant was accused of murder, we included the case in our study.

Clear as this definition is in principle, in practice the criminal records required careful handling. Early modern Anglo-American court procedure, including record keeping, differs from that of modern courts in Britain and the United States. English infanticide trials took place in courts of assize, courts of "life and limb" meeting twice a year in circuits throughout the realm. The judges of these courts were drawn from the king's courts at Westminster—the chief justices, puisine justices, barons of the exchequer and sergeants at law. They sat for two or three days in major market towns in their circuits throughout the realm hearing serious crimes and pronouncing sentences. The "home circuit," for example, included the counties of Essex, Hertford, Kent, Surrey, and Sussex. The city of London and the county of Middlesex were served by a quarter sessions court with special oyer and terminer powers. A clerk accompanied the judges, gathering up the jury lists, indictments, and goal records and endorsing these with the results of trials. Individual trials were brief affairs. Defendants were not represented by counsel except in treason cases (after 1696), and a single trial jury of 12 might hear a dozen cases before retiring to give its verdict. If the grand jury brought in a true bill and the trial jury found the defendant guilty, execution could follow in the next few days. The judge was active throughout the trial, supposedly protecting the legal rights of the accused, instructing the jury in the law, and questioning witnesses himself. A judge could remand a prisoner to gaol in order that more evidence be gathered, stay judgment upon a prisoner to await a royal pardon, or carry a legal question back to the king's bench in Westminster.

The judges passed sentence on the convicted, sending the guilty to pillory, whipping post, gaol, or death on the gallows.

This system was not conducive to extensive trial record keeping. Constantly on the move, often overwhelmed by the work, and occasionally unqualified for the task, the clerks collected papers and recorded decisions hastily. Some names, dates, places, and occupations were erroneously entered. The court records of the assizes are filed at the Public Record Office in London. The best preserved of the Elizabethan assize files are those for the home circuit. The assize files include gaol registers, jury lists, and other papers collected by the clerks.

The crime of bastardy plays an important part in the study of infanticide. Records of bastardy and other lesser crimes, including those committed by infanticide suspects, can be traced through the quarter sessions dockets. The quarter sessions court for a country met four times each year. On its bench were county justices of the peace. Individual justices also sat as magistrates, in which capacity they were often the first officials to hear accusations of infanticide. They had the power to examine and bind over suspects, and to compel witnesses to appear at the assizes. The records of quarter sessions are kept in county record offices and libraries. Of these, the calendared Essex County quarter sessions records are the most accessible. The Middlesex and London court records are also a detailed, extensive and well preserved source of cases. For the latter portion of the seventeenth century, and almost all of the eighteenth century, cases at the London and Middlesex quarter sessions were published in the *Old Bailey Sessions Papers*.

Within the assize records (in Middlesex, the quarter sessions papers) are scattered coroners' inquests. From the time of Norman rule, coroners convened juries of knowledgeable local men to view corpses and determine the cause of death. If the coroner's jury found evidence of foul play, a justice of the peace could order the sheriffs and their deputies to bring the suspect to gaol. When available, the inquest records are often the most detailed accounts of homicides.

A simpler judicial system than that of England makes New England colonial criminal records more accessible than those of the mother country. The seventeenth-century councils and courts of assistants—the upper legislative houses of Massachusetts, Connecticut, and Plymouth—were the first courts of life and limb to appear in those colonies. At the end of the seventeenth century these bodies were replaced by separate courts of superior jurisdiction, staffed by a better trained class of judges (though the line between legislative officeholding and judicial appointment was not fixed until the Revolution). The justices of the colonial superior court and the courts of assistants before them rode circuit in each colony, whenever the dispersal of population precluded the hearing of all cases at the colonial capital. Infanticide accusations came before these high courts. The records of colonial Plymouth are in print. The records of the Massachusetts court of assistants and its successor, the superior court of judicature, are kept at the New Suffolk county court house, Boston. File papers for the cases in the court records are scattered through more than 900 volumes gathered in the court house. Records for county courts in Massachusetts are housed, in the English manner, in the county. The Connecticut state library, in Hartford, has collected the records of the court of assistants and superior court of that colony. File papers are included in this collection, as are microfilms of county court records.

With sources as varied as these, geographic coverage had to be restricted. We concentrated our energies upon Massachusetts, including its "province" of Maine, Plymouth, and Connecticut in the New World, and upon a part of the home circuit and Middlesex in England. The colonies of Rhode Island and New Hampshire did not experience infanticide to any extent, so far as we were able to determine, and their records throw little light upon our subject. Additional English cases and colonial cases from other jurisdictions are introduced as they illuminate the law, social attitudes, or courtroom practices. As it happens, a 1560 case from the county of Chester, on the Welsh border, and an 1803 case from Yorkshire are given special attention because they illustrate vital shifts in official interpretation of the law.

Our quantitative design also restricted geographical scope. First, we wished to have reliable data bases for statistical comparisons. New England records, particularly those of Massachusetts and Connecticut, and the cases recorded in the home circuit counties of Essex, Hertford, and Sussex, as well as Middlesex, were well kept, and reached back to the beginnings of our period. Comparability of data drawn from court records of this type requires that the variations between geographical areas be fully understood. Scholars have noted and probed the differences between New England and the mother country at great length, and we relied upon this scholarship to guide us in framing suitable hypotheses about the causes and handling of infanticide cases in the two regions. At the same time, the manner of defining, recording, and pursuing crime in both jurisdictions was similar enough to permit comparisons between them. Finally, we were concerned with the effects of modernization and social change upon the crime of infanticide and its treatment in the courts. This concern directed our attention to the capital of the empire, London, and its surrounding area, as well as to Massachusetts and Connecticut in the New World.

To be sure, we were also aware that the criminal courts records for the home circuit in England and the New England colonies were the most suited to statistical analysis, although even these records had gaps and mistakes in them. Of course, no criminal courts record can tell the scholar about those crimes which went unreported. Our statistical pictures of indictment rates, conviction percentages, and the characteristics of defendants are built almost entirely upon those cases which came to the courts. The cases we have before us are not really a sample of all the crimes, because we cannot be sure that certain classes of infanticide (for example infanticides among the nobility) went entirely unnoticed. It is because we are primarily interested in the impact of this crime upon the criminal justice system, that is, upon the effects of those cases that were discovered, reported, and tried, that our statistics and statistical methods retain their validity.

Although we employ quantitative analytical techniques, it is not merely the striking fluctuations in indictment and conviction rates that attract the eye to early modern infanticide trials. Other measures are equally telling. When literary entrepreneurs in seventeenth- and eighteenth-century England transcribed and published accounts of trials or other criminal court proceedings, for example, they featured infanticide cases on their cover pages and in their advertisements. Infanticide trials were communal events, as these broadside and pamphlet editors well knew. When infanticides were discovered in New England, clergymen rarely missed the opportunity to lecture on the case and publish their observations after the execution. Massachusetts superior court justices, such as Benjamin Lynde and Samuel Sewall, rarely referred to specific criminal cases in their diaries, but both men mentioned infanticide cases they had encountered.

Although infanticide did not absorb nearly as much of the courts' attention as other capital crimes—for example breaking and entering, in England, or murder of adults, in New England—it was not rare. Over 25 percent of all murders heard in the early modern English courts we have studied were infanticides. If one excludes London (where duels ending in death inflated the number of adult murder victims), infanticides averaged over 30 percent of all early modern English homicide cases. In seventeenth-century Plymouth, one of the three white people executed for killing Europeans was a woman, for the murder of her infant. In neighboring Massachusetts, three of the 11 executions for murder in the seventeenth century involved women, for infanticide. Finally, 90 percent of all murderous assaults by women were directed at infants. No jurisdiction we studied was exempt from the crime or its infamy.

All dates in the following pages have been converted to "new style," the calendar reform adopted in England and her colonies after 1752, in order to avoid confusion. All calculations of rates were done after the conversion of dates. Thus an infanticide committed on March 15, 1701/2 was included in the totals for 1702.

Acknowledgments

Our study of historical records was made possible by the courtesy of the staffs of a number of archives and libraries, the encouragement of other scholars, and generous institutional support. We wish to thank the staffs of the Public Record Office, the Corporation of London Record Office, the Greater London Record Office, the Library of the Institute of Advanced Legal Studies, and the British Library, all in London, the Essex County Record Office, Chelmsford, Essex, the Library of Congress Law Library, and the Folger Shakespeare Library, both in Washington, D.C., the office of the Clerk of the Supreme Judicial Court, New Suffolk County Court House, Boston, the Boston Public Library, the History Library of the State Library, Hartford, Connecticut, the Columbia University Law School Library, the Ohio State University Law School Library, the Ohio Historical Society Library, the University of Notre Dame Memorial Library, the University of Georgia Law School Library, and the Langdell Library of the Harvard University Law School. We are grateful to colleagues who generously aided our efforts. Bradley Chapin, John Langbein, and Daniel Scott Smith read the entire manuscript and offered helpful suggestions. Others, including J. M. Beattie, J. S. Cockburn, John Demos, Eli Faber, Thomas Green, Douglas Greenberg, Richard Jensen, Joseph Lynch, Walter Metzger, Robert Malcolmson, Richard B. Morris, Franklin Pegues, Phillip Resnick, David Rothman, and Robert Wells commented on particular sections. To Harold Hyman and Alden Vaughan, friendly critics and gentle mentors, our debt is immeasurable. William Nelson, our editor, sharpened our thinking and our prose. The directors of the American Philosophical Society and the Newberry Library Family and Community History Center provided essential research grants. Versions of parts of this essay were read to the American Society for Eighteenth Century Studies, the American Society for Legal History, the Columbia University Seminar on Early American History and Culture, the Indiana University/Purdue University American Studies Center conference on Childhood in American Life, the Duquesne History Forum, the Newberry Library Family and Community History Center, the Organization of American Historians, and the Ohio State University History Seminar. We thank the organizers of these sessions for the opportunity to present our ideas. Finally, we wish to thank our spouses for their cooperation and understanding.

Part I

Infanticide and the
Criminal Justice System,
England and New England,
1558-1803

I

The Discovery of Infanticide, England, 1558-1650

Although long practiced in England, infanticide did not become a major concern of royal authorities until the reign of Elizabeth I. That epoch saw a burst of prosecutions and the emergence of new attitudes and laws on the crime. The cause of this shift in practice and opinion lies in a combination of jurisprudential, religious, economic, and social forces. With their confluence begins the history of modern Anglo-American infanticide law.

Premodern England must have experienced some infanticide. The crime is as old as human society and comparative anthropologists have estimated that paleolithic parents may have eliminated as many as 50 percent of their newborn females.[1] In Christian Europe, ecclesiastical courts bore the brunt of these cases. Old and New Testament passages on infant sacrifice led to canon law injunctions against the sin of baby murder. Clerics in England knew this doctrine well. Following Gratian's *Decretium* (1140) and the Decretals of Gregory IX (1234), medieval English ecclesiastical courts like those of Canterbury prescribed severe penance for suspected infanticidal parents. Within the single decade of the 1470s, for example, the Canterbury tribunal heard

and punished culprits in four cases. These included a suspected exposure, a drowning, and two cases of suffocation
by overlaying, the most frequently cited method of infanticide in these courts. Negligent homicide was punished in
the same fashion as premeditated killing, for these courts
demanded penitance for acts, with or without immoral intention. If the defendant pleaded his or her innocence,
neighbors were asked to act as "compurgators" to swear
their faith in the word of the accused, or the defendant
might provide other evidence of innocence. Punishment
from these archdeacon's courts, often called "bawdy courts"
for the volume of sexual offenses which passed before
them, might include self-administered physical abuse,
prayer, and dietary restrictions. They were not courts of life
and limb and could not shed blood.[2]

The king's courts alone could take away life upon conviction for a crime. They heard all cases of homicide, including the murder of infants, but they gave little attention to
the latter crime. From the establishment of royal courts of
criminal justice by the successors of William of Normandy,
through the reign of the first Tudors, there were few cases
and little legal commentary on infanticide. Only a handful
of cases of infant murder in the late medieval files and rolls
show that commissioners in eyre and, later, judges on assize
circuit, encountered occasional accusations of infanticide.
At the Wiltshire eyre of 1249, for example, the hundred of
Chippenham was fined for letting Basilia of Wroxhall flee.
She threw her infant son into a ditch to die, and a dog carried the corpse through the town. Eleven years later, in the
town of Croyden, Aumphelisa and her mother, Matilda, the
widow of William the town clerk, murdered the younger
woman's male infant. Edith Perrycresse heard the child cry
out and raised hue and cry, but the culprits were not arrested. Authorities at the Cambridge assizes fined the town
for letting Aumphelisa and Matilda escape. A handful of
other surviving cases in Oxford, Shropshire, and North-
amptonshire show that persons suspected of infanticide
faced the king's justice.[3]

Surviving records of coroner's inquests, an earlier and

more inclusive stage of the criminal justice system than trials, evidence the same paucity of cases. Coroners were charged with the examination of all corpses, and an inquest into the cause of death of an infant could lead to an indictment for homicide in the king's courts. Yet:

> Infanticide virtually never appeared in either the coroners' rolls or in the trials in gaol delivery. Of 2,933 homicide cases which came before gaol delivery justices in three counties [of Norfolk, Northamptonshire, and Yorkshire] from 1300–48 only one case of infanticide appeared, that of Alice Grut and Alice Grym who were accused of drowning a three day old infant. One suspicious case came into the London coroners' inquests but the child was judged to have died of disease and one infant was found in the river at Oxford which, the jurors said, had floated down the river and they knew nothing further about the death.[4]

The apparent paucity of infanticides is in striking contrast to the number of other kinds of homicide that occurred. In the thirteenth century, there were 321 homicides heard at four Bedford eyres, the forerunners of the assize courts, 382 homicides at two sittings of the commissioners in eyre in Kent, 309 cases for three Oxford eyre meetings, 376 homicides for three Warwick visits by the commissioners, and 199 cases in two eyre sittings in London. Prosecution for homicide was common, but prosecution for infant murder, apparently, was quite rare. The Surrey eyre of 1253, for example, heard only one case of infanticide.[5]

In the absence of positive evidence, one might conclude that few infanticides actually took place. The actual extent of crime—often called the "dark figure"—is a continuing puzzle for criminologists studying offenses far less easily concealed than infanticide. The apparent scarcity of cases in medieval England is nevertheless incompatible with findings from other Western Christian societies. Sixteenth-century Florentine officials reported over 181 suspected cases of infanticide in the years between 1500 and 1540. In the 250 years after 1500, the city of Nuremburg executed 87 young women for infanticide. Genevan authorities brought

25 women to trial for infanticide between 1580 and 1680. Was England different? Examined more carefully, the fragmentary English criminal records from late medieval archives show suggestive incidents of drownings, burnings, and other "accidental" deaths of infants. The few cases that did appear in assize court records closely resembled cases tried on the European continent. It seems reasonable to assume that more infanticide occurred than was prosecuted. Cases must have been hidden from the magistrates or not taken seriously by officials. Neighbors may have refused to assist in the prosecution. Perhaps these cases were simply too difficult to prove. Or some combination of these facts prevented prosecution.[6]

The state of the king's law on the crime through the middle of the sixteenth century demonstrates that infanticide had little salience for English lawmakers, commentators, or justices despite the fact that the general topic of homicide was a subject of interest throughout the late medieval period. Although thirteenth-century commentators Bracton and Fleta referred to neonaticide to illustrate the doctrine that a murder victim must be fully alive for the act of violence to be a homicide, they observed the youth of the victim only as an illustration of the doctine *in rerum natura*. The first manual for justices of the peace, Marowe's 1503 manuscript "De Pace Terre," repeated Bracton's cursory reference on the subject of infant murder. Justice William Stanford's widely cited *Les Plees Del Coron* (1557) also included this note. Among later writers for justices of the peace, Anthony Fitzherbert's, *L'Office et Auctoritie de Justices de Peace* (1538), judged by some later scholars the most authoritative essay of its kind, simply ignored infanticide.[7]

Two later Elizabethan legal texts gave increased attention to infanticide—but only as an example of the technical difference between accessories and principals in murder. Into an 1584 enlargement of Fitzherbert's manual, Richard Crompton, an able legal writer, placed the infanticide case of "Elizabeth P." Some years before, Chief Justice James Dyer (d. 1582) had inserted "Parker's case" into his *Reports*. Elizabeth P's case, which had occurred in 1568, featured the murder of a five-week-old baby by its spinster mother and a male accessory. Both were indicted as principal felons. Although Elizabeth, the mother, was not married, Crompton made no issue of her sexual immorality. The point of the case was that both mother and male accessory were guilty of murder. Dyer's report of "Parker's case" propounded the same point of law. In 1562, George Parker, a clergyman, Jane Saway, a midwife, and Helena Millicent, the recipient of Parker's adulterous advances, conspired to kill Millicent's child when it was born. Saway performed the act, but all were hanged. There was abundant matter for moral censure at every stage of the crime, but the immorality of its actors was not central to Dyer's comment. His point was that all three—midwife, mother, and parson, even though the last named had only abetted the act—were guilty of murder. Crompton and Dyer were defining the culpability of accomplices; neither the age and innocence of the victim nor the moral status of the suspect were important issues.[8]

This situation—few cases and little case law—changed dramatically within the next decade. By the 1580s, cases of infanticide were multiplying in the courts. The numbers of infanticide cases heard by coroners and judges on the home circuit and in Middlesex showed a sharp increase under Elizabeth's reign over previous years.

Table 1.1
Incidence of Newborn Bastard Infant Death
Leading to Indictments of Mother
(from Coroner's Inquests and Indictments), 1558–1593

	1558–1563	1564–1569	1570–1575	1576–1581	1582–1587	1588–1593
Essex	2	4	1	7	5	4
London and Middlesex[a]	1	0	1	2	2	1
Sussex	2	1	2	3	1	5

[a] These figures are surely too small, but the underrecording is probably evenly spread through the entire period. See Chapter 4, pp. 96–97.

The machinery of local criminal justice enforcement had begun to search out and punish infanticide suspects. The figures in Table 1.1 cannot be attributed to mere Tudor population increases, for population in England had been steadily increasing since the plague years of the mid-fourteenth century. Even more striking is the 225 percent jump in cases after 1576. Both the overall and the post-1576 rise in frequency of infanticide cases must be laid in part to magistrates' decisions to prosecute more accusations, as well as coroners' and grand jurors' acceptance of evidence that a homicide had been committed in these cases of suspicious infant death. But what lay behind these new attitudes toward the crime? The appearance of a new case note in a respected and popular manual for justices of the peace gives a clue to this puzzle.[9]

At some time between 1584 and 1593, Richard Crompton decided to insert a reference to an additional infanticide case in his 1593 revision of Fitzherbert's manual. The case occurred in 1560, in the Welsh border shire of Chester. It was hardly a landmark case in its day and Crompton learned of it from an "informed source" by word of mouth. The note read:

> A Harlot is delivered of an infant which she puts alive in an orchard, and covers with leaves; and a kite strikes at him with its talons, from which the infant shortly dies, and she is arraigned for murder, and is executed.
>
> [Authors' translation.]

No innovator, Crompton was probably responding to others' growing interest in this sort of crime. A justice of the peace for Staffordshire himself, he frequented the high courts in Westminster and the prerogative courts that sat across the Great Hall. The sergeants at law and justices, the attorneys who practiced before them, as well as the legal writers like himself, were his sources. His readers were local legal officials. Their task in infanticide cases was to establish the cause of death and the probability of premeditation. The kite case dealt with both of these issues.[10]

First, the kite case offered a technical rule of evidence in infanticide cases that would assist and be appreciated by Crompton's audience. Infant deaths resulting from exposure or neglect presented a thorny problem to legal officials, and Crompton's note had clear utility for them. The defendant in the kite case had neglected to provide proper care for an infant and that fact alone rendered her guilty of murder when the infant died. This straightforward interpretation of the kite case spoke to coroners and justices of the peace faced with the nearly insurmountable task of determining the cause of death of infants and deciding if sufficient evidence existed for a charge of murder. At the coroner's inquest and during the justices' examination of suspects, some of those accused of infanticide must have pleaded guilty of ignorance or neglect in exposing an infant, but denied premeditation. Signs of violence on the victim and witnesses to live birth could establish an intention to kill, but decomposition of concealed infants made medical confirmation of violence almost impossible in that era, and "secret" delivery, a fact often noted in the inquest documents, reduced the chance that anyone would hear the child's first cries. Sixteenth- and seventeenth-century coroners simply could not be sure if a child was born dead and then abandoned, or born alive and exposed.[11]

A series of coroners' inquests in Essex illustrates the uncertainty in fact-finding. On March 11, 1568, Margaret Hilles, an unmarried servant, was cleared by the coroner of complicity in the death of her newborn male bastard. The inquest found the child to be stillborn. Mary Lawrence gave birth to a child in the spring of 1571, and threw the body into a pond. An inquest determined that the infant had been born dead. In 1576, the corner's jury concluded that Katherine Bond had not murdered her newly born male bastard, but that "John Stile"—one of the many alias for an unknown malefactor—had. A contrary result was reached in a 1580 case, when a coroner's jury and a trial jury found spinster Agnes Death guilty of killing her bastard daughter immediately upon its birth, even though the clerk of the assizes noted in the file that "Yt was not directly proved the child was in lyff."[12]

Second, in the kite case the defendant had done more than expose and neglect an infant. She concealed the victim with leaves as well. Concealment brought additional issues before the trial jury. Concealment of a stillborn bastard to avoid "poor law" penalties or ostracism by neighbors was not a felony. The act might well occur to an unmarried servant just delivered of a dead infant or one who died shortly after birth. When an infant was found in a privy vault, concealment might be taken as evidence of murder— or it might not. The rules of evidence in English homicide trials were not sophisticated; indeed, they hardly existed. A trial jury might reach a verdict upon any evidence which satisfied its members. The trial jury was "not bound strictly" even "to the matter and form of the indictment." Some young, ill-tutored mothers did not know when they were pregnant, much less in labor, and their infant might have fallen into a privy by accident, or been placed there after stillbirth. Individual juries made various decisions in privy vault cases. Joan Tacke was committed to prison in London for throwing her newborn down a privy vault, where it lay for three hours before discovery. When it died the next day, the coroner's inquest found her guilty, but a trial jury acquitted her. Mary Cooke, another spinster suspected of murdering her newborn by dropping it into the privy, was found guilty at the Middlesex gaol delivery sessions, and hanged. In the end, coroners' juries and trial juries sometimes found for the defendant, sometimes against her.[13]

Crompton's note also reported a third fact which had evidently been important to the Chester assize jury as they sought to untangle the questions of cause of death and premeditation. He stated that the defendant was a harlot. Her moral reputation must have been relevant to the verdict (why else include it in the note). Her previous known sexual excesses told against her at the assizes, for her immorality implied a disregard for community sanctions and domestic norms. Concealment of her victim was the last of many trespasses secreted from the eyes of the magistrates. So callous and wanton a woman must have been capable of premeditation, of intending that the infant die from exposure or the attack of wild animals. The ill fame of the defendant tied neglect and concealment to premeditation. In a final effort to make this clear, Crompton added the words "with the intent of killing the infant" to his last edition of *L'Office,* published posthumously in 1606.[14]

If Crompton knew his audience's thinking at all, he must have glimpsed the power of such a case note for establishing premeditation. Concealment of sexual transgressions among poor women was a growing concern of Elizabethan and early Jacobean religious and legal spokesmen. At the opening of the semiannual assize court sessions, ministers singled out the "descendents of Eve," especially poorer serving women, as bearers of the temptations of the flesh. The lewdness of these women, described as "naked Bathshebas", was viewed as Satan's way of ruining Christian men. The sexual immorality of lewd women was both a sign and a step toward moral deformity of a more serious nature. Reformation leaders' repugnance to concealment of sin reinforced their condemnation of sexual excess. These ministers believed that sin could not be hidden from an omniscient God; the attempt to conceal it was proof of an unregenerate spirit. The first steps to salvation were sorrow and admission of sin; "always to submit to Christ and his true spokesmen." Though the Devil was everywhere, tempting and trying souls, only the weak and the wanton succumbed. The harlot who concealed her sin was the antithesis of the submissive Christian wife and mother.[15]

As the Reformation progressed in England, the king's justices increasingly encountered women accused of sexual immorality. Under Henry VIII and his successors, royal courts inexorably encroached upon the domestic jurisdiction of the ecclesiastical courts. A large portion of the case loads of the latter concerned accusations of female sexual incontinence. Long familiar with cases of this type, the church courts prescribed moderate penance for offenses. The gradual shift of the agency for punishing many sexual deviations from the church to the royal courts thrust large numbers of disreputable women before magistrates upon charges of fornication, bastardy, and similar crimes. The "harlot" of Crompton's note was no stranger to the justices.[16]

The magistrates' response to these cases was influenced by a momentous social and economic upheaval. As the sixteenth century drew to a close, authorities grew increasingly fearful of the sexual immorality and criminal tendencies of the increasingly numerous wandering poor. While the actual size and mobility of the landless work force may not have been as menacing as officials warned, and the process of enclosure not quite as uniform and disruptive as the poor complained, there can be no doubt that English leaders were frightened. The poor were deemed to be "rogues" and "vagabonds," a drain upon the good people whose parishes the poor invaded. Anxiety and anger mingled in official condemnation of these men and women:

> from the royal physicians concerned about the danger to public health and Bacon appalled at this "seed of peril and tumult in a state" to magistrates and ministers like Lambarde and Perkins who agreed that the laws against vagrants were "grounded upon the laws of God and nature itself." Vagabonds became the scapegoats for all social problems. They were carriers of rumour, sedition, and disease, and they infected others with their "licentious liberty.". . .

In 1577, acerbic scholar William Harrison warned of the criminality of this "rabble":

> What notable robberies, pilferies, murders, rapes, and stealings of young children, burning, breaking, and disfiguring their limbs to make them pitiful in the sight of people, I need not . . . rehearse. . . .

Sexual offenses and abuse of children were prominent in his list. With or without evidence of such heinous crimes, contemporary magistrates and church wardens could see that the vagabonds were desperately poor and that they seemed to travel in gangs. This alone raised the spectre of social disorder washing over the entirety of the kingdom, and flowing as a tide toward London. Lawmakers in nearby Westminster could hardly avoid the spectacle.[17]

Out of the growing concern for social disorder in the country came a spate of "personal control" laws. Elizabethan and early Stuart parliaments regulated the outward signs of disorder and immorality. Drinking, gaming, sabbath solemnity, swearing, dress, alehouse-keeping, and bastardy were all treated by statute. These laws did not seek to uproot the cause of poverty, but to dampen its dangerous effects. The personal conduct laws defined propriety; enforcement was left to the justices of the peace sitting as magistrates in their own jurisdictions or in the quarter sessions. Theirs was the task of discerning and punishing socially unacceptable conduct.[18]

One of these Elizabethan social control laws, 18 Eliz. I, c. 3, (1576), brought infanticide out of the shadows of the criminal law. The "poor law" of 1576 punished parents of bastard children who "defrauded" the parish of its capacity to relieve the "true poor" by thrusting destitute infants upon local charity. The mother was to name the father, and the father was to give a bond or weekly payment to the parish. Noncompliance could result in corporal punishment and gaol terms for either parent. Poor mothers almost always faced public disgrace under this act. Fathers drawn from the landless laboring class fled; well-to-do-fathers, on occasion the masters of the unwed mother, disputed her accusation of paternity. The position of the justice of the peace in these cases was unenviable, and parliament chastised local officials for ineptitude. Seven James I, c. 4 (1609), "An Act for the due execution of divers Laws Statutes heretofore made against rogues, vagabonds, sturdy beggars, and other lewd and idle persons" demanded that justices better organize their efforts against the wandering lascivious poor. Bastardy was singled out in this law as a "great dishonor" and "great charge" to the nation.[19]

Even without official prodding, enforcement of the poor

law had become a major concern of the justices. In the
quarter sessions, where bastardy cases were heard, justices
enforced the strictures of 18 Eliz. I, c. 3. William Lambarde,
a justice of the peace for the county of Kent and a legal
scholar, inveighed against "dissolute living" and "lewd and
deceitful practices" when he routinely ordered "the whipping of Abigail Sherwood for a bastard man child born by
her at Chatham" and sent her to the house of correction.
After 1576, Lambarde and other justices were faced with a
rising tide of bastardy cases. By the 1590s, bastardy cases
were flooding the sessions courts throughout the realm.
Historians of the Hampshire, Somerset, and Lincolnshire
sessions agree that for sheer volume alone bastardy was the
"single measure" most difficult for the justices to handle.
Forced to cajole confessions from pregnant women and
compliance from recalcitrant fathers of bastards, the justices
must have found these cases tests of their patience and authority.[20]

The case load itself was not the only burden. Each case
was liable to return to the court two or three times, from the
initial examination of the mother to determine the father's
identity, to the warrant for the father to come to court,
through repeated demands that defaulting fathers pay the
parish for care of the child. A number of men might be
named as the father, and any one of them might actually
have been the father—leading to charges and counter-
charges and throwing an entire community into turmoil.
Examination of the Essex quarter sessions records from
1576 through 1624 shows that about 25 percent of all bastardy cases involved more than one court order even after
fatherhood was established. Some defendants, like Edmund
Cheveley, "alias Lacey," openly defied the magistrates. On
January 1579, Susan Dates confessed to a midwife, in the
midst of her delivery of a bastard child, that Cheveley was
its father. Cheveley was called to court and on April 30,
1579, agreed to pay 6d. weekly for upkeep of his bastard
son. He was recalled to the court on July 2, 1579, and again
on June 30, 1580, and both times refused to appear. It was

clear the he had reneged on his oath. Cheveley's unwillingness to pay Buttesbury parish went unpunished, though he
was cited in the court records as an obnoxious and bawdy
man.[21]

The poor law of 1576 required justices of the peace to examine women accused of bastardy. Tremendous moral and
legal pressure was exerted on these women to reveal the
name of the child's father, so that the parish could force
him to support the destitute infant. Midwives were enjoined
to ask the mother in labor for this information. Depositions
of these examinations filed with the court records illustrate
the complexity and tension of bastardy cases. On April 2,
1589, depositions were collected in the case of spinster Margery Hawles:

2 *April, A.D.1589.*

Examined on behalf of the plaintiff. [Bastardy cases had a civil side as well as a crimi-nal side, and are mixed in with the civil and public business of the quarter ses-sions.]

Margaret Pullyn, wife of Henry Pullyn of "Gaines Coulne", the midwife, Joan, wife of Walter Newman, and Audrey, wife of Morrice Hurrell of Earls Colne, upon their oaths taken before Is-rael Amies and Anthony Maxey, esquires.

These examinants say that they demanded of Margery
Hawles, in the time of her travail, who was in truth the father
of her child, "as she woulde aunsweare yt before God and
hope to obteyne his favoure and mercy" who said "God willing soe she woulde, for she woulde bely noe man"; whereupon she said that it was John Stebbing's of Stambourne, her
late master, and no other's but only his.

And further the said Joan Newman did carefully examine
her before her said travail, who then answered her as afterwards she did in her said travail, whereupon this examinant
said unto her "what a gracles and faythless wench art thoue
unto thie dame dwelling in hir howse, for to doe (so) fowle a
fact with thye mr [master]." Who said that he had been enticing her to this folly a year or thereabouts, and that she said
to this examinant that he told the said Margery that he knew

his wife should not live long, and then after her death he would marry her, in recompense to have his will.

And further the said Margery told this examinant that the said John proffered her twenty nobles to charge some other man to father her said child.

Margaret Hawles, wife of Robert Hawles of Chappel Parish and sister of Margery Hawles, taken as above.

Who says that presently after Braintree Fair, the day certainly she remembreth not, the said John Stebbinge came to her house, where Margery Hawles was, and in the presence of this examinant he gave her 4s. with these words, that if he knew where she might be well kept he would pay for her charges and take away the child when it was born.

And further says that within some five or six days after, the said John met this examinant, the said Margery and her father-in-law in a meadow in the parish of Toppesfield, and there amongst other speeches he did utterly deny to this examinant that he was father unto the said Margery's child, but at the coming of the said Margery, and in the presence of this examinant, he took her by the hand and confessed that he had carnally to do with her with these words to wit "That yf thoue hadest made me privye yt [that] thoue hadest bene wth childe, before yt hadd been commonly knowen, I woulde have placed ye and sene ye well kept, in sutche secret mannor yt [that] yt shoulde not have been blassed abrod as nowe yt is."

And also says that the said John did tender unto John Blithe her father-in-law twenty nobles to discharge him of the child of the said Margery, to be paid the Wednesday following at the Widow Browne's house in Bumpstead.

And moreover says that at his first being at her house, the said Margery and he being in a chamber together and this examinant being in the next room adjoining thereunto, she heard the said John tell the said Margery that he would give her five pounds and take away the child and discharge the other charges.

William Rust of Felstead, clerk, taken before the same on 2 May, 1589.

Who say that he, being desired by the wife of Robert Bigg of Felsted, demanded of Margery Hawles her servant whether she were with child or no, for that it was so commonly reported, whereupon she confessed that she was with child, and that John Stebbing her late master was the father thereof, and none but he only had to do with her, which was very often.

"And I burdininge her very muche, she aunsweared me she would never slaunder any, nor say yt [that] any other had to doe with hir yt [that] she should dye for yt, for yf she did she said she should offend greatly," and this she confessed unto him in the month of September, 1588.

This one case entailed ten more witnesses' testimony before it was completed—all prior to the first court appearance of the supposed father.[22]

Proceedings like these accustomed justices to accusations of bastardy, and ultimately to suspicions of infanticide when a newborn bastard died. The severity of the poor laws could drive unwed mothers to the latter act. With the same force that the poor law urged magistrates to ferret out bastardy among the poor and punish it severely, the law counselled the poor to conceal bastardy pregnancy and perhaps to murder their bastard newborns. If the defendant could conceal the pregnancy and delivery, she might hope to dispose of a dead bastard infant and avoid the penalties of 18 Eliz I, c. 3. Infrequent changes of garb and the frequency of female indispositions other than pregnancy permitted concealment of child bearing. And concealment, in turn, sometimes ended when unwed mothers "secretly gave birth," and "without the feelings of motherhood" dispatched their infants to the other world.[23]

The heightened pressure upon authorities to find and punish bastardy among the poor and the increased incentive that the law gave the poor to perform infanticide increased the yearly number of mothers indicted for the crime of bastard neonaticide after 1576. Table 1.1 showed a small, steady number of indictments before the poor law, and a distinctly larger, fairly constant yearly frequency after 1576. After the poor law, indictments for infanticide in the counties examined showed a 225 percent increase. The numbers are too small to have universal significance, but they tend to confirm the impact of the poor law.

Neither the swelling of all types of criminal indictments at the assizes nor the rise of population in the 1580s and 1590s can explain this jump in infanticide cases. It is true that between 1570 and 1600, all criminal business before the assizes grew 250 percent. The largest component of this increase were crimes against property, rather than crimes of violence. While infanticide has some relation to economic need (see Chapter 5), it is very unlike robbery, burglary, and grand larceny. Other crimes, far closer to infanticide in form, including the murder of adults, did not rise nearly so precipitously. Population growth cannot explain this abrupt climb in the number of infanticide cases. About 8000 people each year augmented the population of Tudor London. Middlesex population was mounting as well. Essex increased from 35,000 adults in the reign of Elizabeth to twice that number a century later. Sussex population must have been advancing, if only in the Southwark docks area on the Thames. The steady small increments in population would trace a curvilinear path for rising infanticide cases were the two phenomena closely related, not the steplike progression in the latter that one finds.[24]

The explanation for the jump in indictments lies in the operation of the criminal justice system. Bastard neonaticides constituted over 70 percent of all murders of infants under nine years of age in the records. Concealment of pregnancy is mentioned in 55 percent of these cases. The former were the cases which the poor laws pushed in front of justices of the peace. Detection of these cases improved because justices and their informants sought out bastardy. The defendants in these cases fit the typology in Crompton's note.

One final piece of evidence attests to the increased sensitivity of the courts to the connection between bastardy and motivation for infanticide after 1576. This is the rate of conviction for infanticide before and after the poor law. If the argument above is correct, the latter should exceed the former. In the 17 years before 18 Eliz I, c. 3 (1576), Essex assize court juries found two mothers of five tried for bastard neonaticide to be guilty. In the 17 years after the poor law, juries found nine of 13 guilty. In Sussex, the figures for the same period before the poor law were three guilty of five tried, but seven were guilty of nine brought to trial in the 17 years after the poor law. By the time—1593—that Crompton wrote about the kite case, the change in justices' and juries' attitudes was becoming clear. His citation mirrored the alteration in views of this crime.

Crompton's note would become a guiding rule in manuals and commentaries. In 1619, Michael Dalton referred to the kite case in his immensely popular handbook for justices of the peace:

> A Harlot deliured of a childe, hidde it in an Orchard (it being alive) and couered it with leaves, and a Kite stroke at it, and the childe dyed therof, and the mother was arraigned and executed for Murder.

Chief Justice Matthew Hale's *Pleas of the Crown* (1682) cited the kite case, and it later made its way into Blackstone and Hawkins. Other manuals for justices of the peace, including Bond's *A Compleat Guide for Justices of Peace* (1707) and Burn's *Justice of Peace and Parish Officer* (1845), adopted the reference. In 1877, Sir James Stephen at last put the harlot's shame to rest with the argument that the kite was no longer so dangerous in England as to require a mother to guard against it.[25]

With or without Crompton's effort, magistrates and juries were increasingly labelling "immoral" women as potential defendants for child murder and trying more of their suspected infanticides in the courts. A definitive statutory statement on the concealment of bastardy neonaticide was shortly forthcoming. In 1624, parliament passed a law guiding juries in bastard neonaticide cases. The new law did not define a crime—the murder of a newborn child was no more or less a murder than before—but the Jacobean infan-

ticide statute codified the precepts and precedent implicit in
the kite case note. Chapter 27 of the statute of 21 James I
read:

> An act to prevent the destroying and murthering of bastard
> children.
>
> WHEREAS, many lewd women that have been delivered of
> bastard children, to avoid their shame, and to escape punish-
> ment, do secretly bury or conceal the death of their children,
> and after, if the child be found dead, the said woman do
> alledge, that the said child was born dead; whereas it falleth
> out sometimes (although hardly it is to be proved) that the
> said child or children were murthered by the said women,
> their lewd mothers, or by their assent or procurement:
>
> II. For the preventing therefore of this great mischief, be
> it enacted by the authority of this present parliament, That if
> any woman after one month next ensuing the end of this
> session of parliament be delivered of any issue of her body,
> male or female, which being born alive, should by the laws of
> this realm be a bastard, and that she endeavour privately,
> either by drowning or secret burying thereof, or any other
> way, either by herself or the procuring of others, so to con-
> ceal the death thereof, as that it may not come to light,
> whether it were born alive or not, but be concealed: in every
> such case the said mother so offending shall suffer death as
> in case of murther, except such mother can make proof by
> one witness at the least, that the child (whose death was by
> her so intended to be concealed) was born dead.[26]

The language of the statute hints at its origins: a concern
for the technical problems of evidence and a tone of moral
censure. The statute was concerned with evidentiary difficulties in proving premeditation in a homicide. The preamble of the act reported the courts' inability to determine
whether concealed death was a misprision of murder. The
parenthetical phrase, "although it is hardly to be proved,"
indicated the lawmakers were responding to the practical
difficulties of trying cases of concealed infant death. Pressure from the courts for statutory assistance as the number

of cases grew may have urged dispatch and rigor on the lawmakers.

After the late sixteenth-century surge in indictments for infanticide, the crime came regularly before assize courts, and the number of cases coming before the justices on assize might well have influenced the course of legislation in parliament. Computation of a true "crime rate" from court records is impossible because the crime was easily hidden. Population calculations are equally imprecise. Nevertheless it is possible to construct an estimated "indictment rate." In the 1610s, Greater London high courts had 2.7 indictments for infanticide per year for a population of between 175,-000 and 225,000. This gives an indictment rate of approximately 1.35 per hundred thousand people per year. Elizabethan Essex assize courts averaged about one case per year, for a population of 70,000 adults and children, resulting in a 1.44 per hundred thousand rate. Not all of the population in these calculations was "at risk" to suffer infanticide—perhaps one-third of the total population was under the age of nine—and any computation of a true crime rate would have to deal with this fact. Even if one cannot directly approach the crime rate from the indictment rate, one can speculate (as magistrates might have) about the number of cases escaping justice. From the evidence of Terling parish, Essex, between 1558 and 1650, Keith Wrightson proposes that up to two-and-one-half times as many more neonaticides occurred than were included in records of the criminal courts. Whatever the actual rate of the crime might have been, the number of cases coming to court was large enough to keep the crime before the eyes of authorities. In Hertfordshire and Sussex, as well as Essex, the assizes saw an average of one case of infanticide during each hurried, two- or three-day meeting. Middlesex and London sessions judges saw one and one-half more cases each year than did the home circuit justices. When it did come to court, infanticide often caused a sensation. (If ballads and broadsides are to be believed; see Chapter 4.) One may suppose, moreover, that a very few cases in each jurisdiction might have had a cumulative effect on the imagination of judicial officials, for the same officials went on the assize circuit year after year.[27]

The stridency of the preamble to the law suggests a second, less technical concern. The moral tone of the Jacobean infanticide law is accusatory and unrelenting. "Lewd women" and "lewd mothers" are the targets of the statute. The preamble condemned sexual promiscuity almost as much as murder, and the law applied only to mothers of bastards. Examination of the bill's passage through parliament suggests Puritan interest in its language, although the evidence for this is inferential. Bills to prevent the murder of bastard children were raised in the parliaments of 1607 and 1610 and dropped. References to these bills in the commons *Journals* do not give their provisions, nor the causes of their abbreviated careers. The parliament of 1624, which finally passed the act, had in its previous year's sittings been concerned with Prince Charles' proposed Spanish marriage and the religious war in Germany. Without notice in any of the major diaries of the day, the infanticide act passed through its three readings at the end of the long, wearying session of 1623/4. Nevertheless, between the introduction of the bill on April 17, 1624 and its engrossment on May 27th, a committee of the house of commons heard proposed amendments. That committee of 21 members included William Lytton, Francis Barrington, George Moore, and Alexander St. John, acknowledged leaders of the Puritan party, and Thomas Grimes and Nathaniel Rich, who leaned in that direction. Puritan participation in this committee was only equalled by their interest in sabbath day laws. Puritan influence in parliamentary legislation had grown since Elizabeth's reign, and they had a major role in formulating the personal conduct laws. Puritans in the parliament of 1624 continued to guide the course of legislation: "Immediately after prayers were concluded on the first day of business, it became apparent that the Puritan element in the commons was determined to make itself heard." Puritans feared the concealment of a "hardened heart," the sinfulness of women, and the immorality of the idle. Infanticide would be an abhorrent crime to them. The infanticide law, with its uncompromising attack upon promiscuity, attracted their support.[28]

The Stuart infanticide law enabled courts to establish guilt on the basis of circumstantial evidence of conealment and prior sexual misconduct. The Essex assize returns show the expediency of the new legislation. After 1624, indictments specified the illegitimacy of victims, alerting jurors to the new law. For the 12-year span between 1610 and 1622, three unwed mothers were prosecuted for the death of their newborns, compared to 13 in the 12 years from 1625 to 1637. In the period before the statute, there were two convictions and one acquittal on the charge of murder, approximately the same ratio as the seven convictions and three acquittals for the murder of legitimate or older children in the same years. In the period after the law, there were 11 convictions and two acquittals for crimes fitting the letter of the statute—as opposed to the six not guilty and four guilty verdicts in cases to which the 1624 law did not apply.[29]

In Essex, from 1576 to 1623, there was a positive but weak relationship between guilty verdicts and the guidelines incorporated in the infanticide law, to wit, a newborn bastard victim and its mother as defendant. Out of all infanticide cases, 31 ended in guilty verdicts, and 23 in acquittals. Among those fitting the conditions which would be stipulated in the infanticide law of 1624, 18 cases ended in conviction, and 11 in not-guilty verdicts. Juries hearing cases of married suspects or older victims found about as often for the defendant (12 times) as for the king (13 times).

The association between guilty verdicts and the illegitimacy of the victims in neonaticides grew discernably after the passage of the 1624 statute. Of 39 suspects indicated, 34 were brought to trial. Five escaped from custody. Of

Table 1.2
Verdict by Hypothetical Appropriateness of the
1624 Infanticide Statute, Essex, 1576–1623[a]
Would the Case Have Fit the Statute?

Verdict	Yes	No	
Guilty			
Actual count	18	13	31
Row percentage	58.1	41.9	56.4%
Column percentage	62.1	50.0	
Total percentage	32.7	23.6	
Acquitted			
Actual count	11	12	23
Row percentage	47.8	52.2	41.8%
Column percentage	37.9	46.2	
Total percentage	20.0	21.8	
Other			
Actual count	0	1	1
Row percentage	0.0	100.0	1.8%
Column percentage	0.0	3.8	
Total percentage	0.0	1.8	N=
	29	26	55
	52.7%	47.3%	100.0%

[a] Cramer's $V = .175$.

those tried whose crimes fit the statute, 72.7 percent were convicted. Of those to whom the new law did not apply, 33.3 percent were found guilty.

The increase in positive association from the first cross-tabulation (Table 1.2) to the second (Table 1.3) suggests that the statute had its designated effect upon juries. The violence of the crime was not what influenced jurors, as one sees by comparing infanticide convictions with convictions in murders of adults. In the 19 years from 1603 to 1622 for which the Essex assizes files are fairly complete, 28 cases of murder and manslaughter not involving infants ended in guilty verdicts, 22 ended in acquittals, and seven have an unclear disposition in the record. The last category includes cases in which the culprit was still at large, the record only

Table 1.3
Verdict by Appropriateness of the
Infanticide Statute, Essex, 1625–1648.[a]
Does the Case Fit the Statute?

Verdict	Yes	No	
Guilty			
Actual count	16	4	20
Row percentage	80.0	20.0	58.8%
Column percentage	72.7	33.3	
Total percentage	47.1	11.8	
Acquitted			
Actual count	6	8	14
Row percentage	42.9	57.1	41.2%
Column percentage	27.3	66.7	
Total percentage	17.6	23.5	N=
	22	12	34
	64.7%	35.3%	100.0%

[a]Phi = .382 Significant at the 97.35 percent level (by Fisher exact probability test).

includes the verdict of the coroner's inquest, or the record fails to mention a verdict. In the 19 years from 1624 to 1644, 24 cases ended in conviction, 17 in not guilty verdicts, and 15 were unclear. There is no demonstrable difference between the figures before and after 1624. Against this background, one can see the effect that the infanticide law had upon convictions for fatal crimes of violence by "wanton" women. A fact which had once made conviction for infanticide difficult, concealment, worked after 1624 to hang suspects, because it proved their capacity and willingness to hide sin from their superiors. The high percentage of guilty verdicts after 1624 for bastard neonaticide shows that few accused slipped through the clutches of the statute. The law lent itself to vigorous prosecution of suspects. An authoritative reading of the statute came from Justice John Kelyng, sitting with the Middlesex quarter sessions on the 1662 case of Ann Davis. She was accused of murdering her newborn bastard, and the statute was read. The justice de-

cided "the statute declareth that where the Child is concealed, it shall be taken to be born alive, and if it be dead it
shall be taken, that it was murdered," unless, of course, witnesses testified that it was born dead. Davis was convicted
and sentenced to death.[30]

Although the 1624 statute was punitive and expedient, it
was not a total departure from English precedent. Seventeenth-century lawyers, with the single exception of the
commentator Zachary Babington, saw nothing untoward in
it. A century later, jurists began to call the infanticide law a
reversal of traditional English criminal principles. William
Blackstone thought the statute "savors pretty strongly of severity" and was clearly pleased that in his own century the
burden of proof that the child was born alive had shifted
back to the prosecution. More recently, Sir Leon Radzinowicz has argued that the presumption of guilt, however mitigated in subsequent years, was "an offense against the common law." Nevertheless, the statute's provisions were
neither novel nor quite reversed the general presumption
of the innocence of the accused. They entailed a return to
earlier definitions of the crime of murder. Concealment of
death was a crime in itself as early as Saxon times. It was
proscribed in *morth*, the Saxon law of murder, and the
proscription was repeated in the earliest forms of the Norman *lex murdrum*. To conceal or refuse to reveal the presence of a corpse was a capital offense. The relationship between concealment and secret murder was antiquated in
common law by 1624, but not dead. While the possibility
that Stuart lawmakers had reached back to very old precedents to find a solution to the concealment of bastard infant
death cannot be established, the parallel remains. The general presumption of innocence had not at any rate been destroyed. Dalton instructed that, in "secret murders . . . half
proofs are to be allowed." The statute shifted the burden of
proving a border condition, concealment. Some but not all
of the burden of proof passed to the defense.[31]

In the wake of the statue, the infanticide indictment rate
also rose. Statutory pronouncements may leave the rate of

a crime unchanged, while powerfully affecting the rate of prosecution. The poor law of 1576 shifted social and economic boundaries enough to create a new class of potential infanticidal offenders but the infanticide statute of 1624 was not the same kind of law. The fourfold increase in prosecution of infanticide cases immediately after 1624 was due to increased vigilence on the part of magistrates. The statute brought the act of concealment of infant death over that often vague dividing line between socially tolerated and criminally objectionable acts.

In indictment rates and conviction rates one reads the combination of official aims and community consesus the roots of which reached to the very foundations of social life. The emerging law of infanticide had a place in the larger context of English life. At the very same moment in English history that parliament and the crown struggled to establish their dominion in the moral universe, local communal institutions and customs, which had acted as a buffer between the individual and the power of government, were undergoing transformation. A veritable agrarian "revolution" was undermining relationships between neighbors throughout the realm, with important consequences for infanticide suspects. Population pressures, the bleak harvest years of the 1590s, the continuing flow of poor laborers across the face of the land, and the continuing threat of further displacement of people from their small holdings, put a terrible strain on established forms of charity, wage laboring, and extended community responsibility. The resulting "disruption of basic trust" led neighbor to bring charges against neighbor in the king's courts, which earlier generations had kept within the confines of the community. Infanticide allegations bespoke this breakdown of community. One can still feel the venom in Alice Crewe's allegation that Ann Davis, a neighbor, was "a whore" and "she had three children and murdered them all." A Middlesex justice had to bond Crewe to keep the peace. The ill feeling of neighbors could fall upon a suspect even after acquittal on charges of infanticide. In July 1564, an Essex assize jury found Katherine Collyns of Birchange not guilty of murdering her newborn female infant. A year later, the quarter sessions court in the county had to restrain Oliver Frog, a gentleman, and John Woodcock, of nearby Maunden, "from illegally taking property from William Collyn (Collyns) of Byrchange, husbandman, on the false assumption that the goods were attained because Katherine, wife of the said William, was arrested and imprisoned for the suspected murder of her infant child before baptism but she was not convicted nor attained."[32]

The mechanism by which the community labelled the young unwed mother as dangerous, and thereby played its part in increasing infanticide indictments and convictions, may be explored by analogy to another crime—witchcraft. "The law and conscience of Europe in the sixteenth century vented its force upon old women and unwed mothers." The witch, like the poor, wandering unwed mother, lived at the edge of society. Both had the aura of sexual license about them. The crimes of both were concealed, and often were directed against children. A full quarter of all the indictments brought against witches in England from the fourteenth through the eighteenth century was for bewitching infants. Sixty-two percent of all those accused of witchcraft were believed to have acted at least once against children. Perhaps the most telling similarity of the two crimes in the Tudor era is that both infanticide and witchcraft became objects of royal law and royal prosecution at about the same time. Accusations of witchcraft, like suspicions of overlaying, were by custom heard in the church courts. In 1563, divining by magic and casting spells were made "pleas of the crown" punishable by death.[33]

In the years after Elizabeth's accession, royal courts responded to allegations of the two crimes in very similar fashion. When fears of one rose, accusations of the other increased correspondingly. For example, infanticide and witchcraft indictments in Essex between 1563 and 1623 rose and fell in harmony. The same pattern is found in Middlesex, between 1613 and 1618.

Table 1.4
Infanticide and Witchcraft in Essex, 1558–1623[a]

Period	Infanticide[b]	Witchcraft
1558–1562	3	2
1563–	5	14
1568–	1	13
1573–	4	18
1578–	9	31
1583–	10	44
1588–	4	33
1593–	5	13
1598–	6	15
1603–	3	9
1608–	6	9
1613–	4	4
1618–	3	3

[a] $R^2 = .55$; $b = .15$. Significant at the 99 percent level.
[b] All cases.

We limited the first test of our hypothesis about the labelling of female deviance to 1623 to avoid the jump in infanticide cases resulting from the passage and enforcement of 21 James I c.27. We used figures for both crimes that included coroner's inquests in addition to true bills from

Table 1.5
Infanticide and Witchcraft in Middlesex, 1613 and 1618[a]

Period	Infanticide	Witchcraft
March 1613–August 1613	1	0
September 1613–	4	4
March 1614–	4	4
September 1614–	3	1
March 1615–	1	1
September 1615–	1	0
March 1616–	3	2
September 1616–	1	1
March 1617–	2	1
September 1617–	2	2

[a] $R^2 = .76$, $b = .75$. Significant at the 90 percent level.

grand juries, because we were interested in cases that neighbors and local authorities, not merely assize justices and
their criminal juries, thought ought to be investigated. The
former were more numerous than the latter, for the grand
jury was concerned with evidence and not mere rumor.
Even if it is true that the statute inflated indictment rates of
infanticide after 1624, we can nevertheless test the strength
of the relationship after that time. When we perform this
regression for Essex witchcraft indictments from 1624 to
1648 with infanticide indictments for the same period, we
find an $R^2 = .01$, a slope of .45, and a significance that fails
to meet standard requirements. The slope is comparable to
our earlier results, but since we do not see one of these variables as a "dependent" variable, this information is not so
useful. The small size of the R^2 figure may be due to the
sudden jump in witchcraft indictments after Matthew Hop-
kins' investigations in Essex county, disturbing the labelling
mechanisms of female crime.

Taken literally, tables 1.4 and 1.5 show that witchcraft
was four times as potent an influence upon the number of
infanticide trials in Middlesex as it was in Essex, but this
would be too fine an interpretation of the slopes (b coefficients) of the regressions. It suffices to say that in both
countries the relationships are positive. More important, the
covariance (R^2) of the two crimes is very high. The atmosphere of suspicion and anger against women on the fringes
of the community—old women who demanded but did not
get charity and young women who bore children out of
wedlock—led to increased numbers of charges of witchcraft
and infanticide respectively. One of these crimes did not
cause the other, but when neighbors were stirred to report
and magistrates to prosecute one, the same tended to hap-
pen with the other.[34]

Behind the tide of witchcraft and infanticide prosecutions
one finds the collapse of older, self-contained communities.
Ill feeling toward female neighbors, and more important,
the bringing of such feelings to the king's justices of the
peace, suggest that some defendants acted as scapegoats.

Unwed infanticide suspects played a role, not just as targets for frustration and anger, but as a living definition of the boundary of unacceptable deviance. The young, unwed suspects in infanticide cases whose indictment and convinction rates rose after the poor laws and still more after the infanticide statute, had ignored social norms and official pronouncements too flagrantly. While some of these women were guilty as charged, the additional numbers of them convicted only upon proof of concealment show the force of the social judgments of superiors and neighbors sitting as judges and juries.[35]

2

Infanticide in the Sanctuary of Puritanism New England, 1630-1730

The English settlers of Massachusetts, Plymouth, and Connecticut brought with them the crime of infanticide. Bewildered, angry, and shaken, Puritan magistrates recorded and judged cases of child murder within the New England settlements. Infanticide did not shock the leaders of New England because of its violence or the youth of its victims—John Winthrop and others were likely to have seen or heard of cases in England—but because it augured an uncertain furture for their mission. For Winthrop and his followers, the creation of a "Citty on a Hill" in America was God's errand. His works were everywhere, and at all times to be searched for His purpose. The commission of infanticide within His sanctuaries, just as the occurrence of a monstrous birth or a sudden storm, was a reminder of the sinfulness and frailty of humanity. Before he set foot on the new land, Winthrop warned "if we shall neglect the observacion of these Articles which are the ends wee haue propounded . . . the Lord will surely breake out in a wrathe against vs . . . be revenged of such a perjured people and make us knowe the price of the breach of such a covenant." For the first three generations of New England leaders, infanticide trials were a somber omen of human weakness and divine displeasure.[1]

The study of infanticide in New England is more than illustrative of the Puritans' struggle against a crime; it permits the retesting of assumptions in Chapter 1 about the impact of religion and social norms upon criminal activity and court procedures. Comparison between England and New England affirms the persistent influence of culture despite environmental change, the continuity between English views of infanticide and the colonists' handling of infanticide accusations.

Massachusetts and Connecticut were similar enough in social customs and criminal precepts to the mother country to make comparison possible and yet different enough to make comparison worthwhile. Much is known about these similarities and differences, particularly in social life and legal institutions, affording the student of crime and criminal law some control over differences between the Old World and the New. Some of these differences are striking. There was more participation, more dispersion of power, and hence more control over one's own life in New England than the settlers had known in their former home. New economic opportunities existed for the skilled, the adventurous, and the persevering among the settlers; "the ones who stayed and cultivated cunning, in turning their advantageous situation to account . . . acquired a sense of self-importance and worth in the course of doing so."[2]

Nevertheless, even as they set about building new lives for themselves, the settlers of New England remained loyal to English social and· economic customs, domestic habits, and, above all, English law. The ruling social ideals of the community still echoed those of the mother country. Society remained "a unit, bound together by inviolable ties . . . an organism." Order and subordination were the watchwords of ministers, educators, and magistrates. In custom, conduct, and law, subordination was particularly forced upon women and children. In all of life's duties, "The colonial dame remained subject to her husband's authority." The deviant woman—scold, husband beater, libeller, or worse—

was severely treated. The pillory, ducking stool, and if all else failed, the noose, were the fate of unrepentant women. For the child, parental love was mixed with severe discipline, admonition, and rigor. Children learned to read with the words "In Adam's fall, we sinned all"; a doctrine the magistrates upheld in practice as well as theory. In manners and morals, New England clung to its English traditions.[3]

Although some innovations were made, the force of tradition predominated in criminal law and procedure in New England. Future migrants to New England had been exposed to a wide variety of law and law courts in the realm, and the administration of criminal justice in the borough and courts leet, the quarter sessions of the county, and the solemn progressions of the assizes, was carried into New England criminal law courts. The leaders of the New England settlements were familiar with English courts. A former justice of the peace for the English county of Suffolk, Winthrop understood the roles of the quarter sessions, assizes, and the king's high courts in Westminster. Even to the commonest of the migrants, the majesty of English criminal law would have been revealed through local justices summoning offenders to their presence, levying fines, and binding over suspects to gaol. The discretion and power that English local justices held, New England legal officials retained. In seventeenth-century New England, the upper house of the legislature sat as a court of assistants to hear cases of life and limb, corresponding in function to courts of assize in the mother country. By the end of the seventeenth century, the quasilegislative New England court of assistants had been replaced by a separate judicial institution, bearing the title superior of court of judicature. Hearing and determining capital offenses passed from the assistants to the judges of the superior court.[4]

The common and statutory criminal law of England was also known to the colonists, and what is more was used. According to Bradley Chapin:

One did not need access to the *Statutes of the Realm* to be aware of the laws of parliament. At the local level, the justices of the peace staggered under the load of statutory law. Texts such as Michael Dalton's *Countrey Justice* and William Lambarde's *Eirenarcha*, known to be available in the colonies, bristled with citation of statutory authority. Appended to Lambarde's text is a table of 279 statutes, "verie neare all," that affected the justices of the peace.

In Massachusetts, Plymouth, and Connecticut, English law and precedents on serious crime were known and applied.[5]

Despite surface differences, New England homicide law was substantially the same as English homicide law. Although the codes of Massachusetts (1641, 1648) and Connecticut (1642, 1650) defined serious offenses in biblical terms, with biblical citations, instead of English case and statute, their substance was the same as the English law. The Massachusetts *Body of Liberties* classed homicide among the capital offenses: "4: If any person shall commit any wilful MURTHER, which is Man slaughter, committed upon premeditate malice, hatred, or crueltie not in a mans necessary and just defense, nor by meer casualty against his will, he shall be put to death. Exod. 21.12.12 Numb. 35.31. 5: If any person slayeth another suddenly in his ANGER, or CRUELTY of passion, he shall be put to death. Levit. 24:27. Numb. 35.20.21. 6: If any person shall slay another through guile, either by poysoning, or other such devilish practice, he shall be put to death. Exod. 21.14." Items 4 and 6 conformed to common law. The last of these provisions may have even harkened back to the early Norman definition of a murder as an ambush already discussed in connection with infanticide in Chapter 1. Premeditation defined murder in England, and Nathaniel Ward, the drafter of the Massachusetts code, "borrowed" these notions from the "common law of England." The Connecticut code of 1650, based upon the Hartford laws of 1642 and the appropriate sections of the Massachusetts codes, used the same language as sections 4 and 6 of the latter.[6]

Item five in the Massachusetts codes discussed a crime that would be called "manslaughter" in England, and would have been punished there with branding for a first offense if a defendant could obtain "benefit of clergy" by reading the 51st or "neck" psalm. The Bay Colony code instead employed the biblical death penalty for killing in the heat of passion. Plymouth contented itself with prescribing death for "wilful murder." This apparent difference between the New England and English concepts of manslaughter did not last long. Massachusetts changed its laws in 1692 to conform homicide without premeditation to the English conception of manslaughter "upon sudden heat." In 1672, Connecticut removed killing in the heat of anger from the list of capital offenses and in 1719 adopted the English punishment for manslaughter. Even before the reduction of penalty in 1692, manslaughter convictions in Massachusetts led to only one hanging; all the others ended with corporal punishment and fines. Although killing in the heat of passion was a capital offense in Massachusetts, its judges treated actual cases as though they had the English law of manslaughter before them.[7]

The other difference between New England capital codes on homicide and the English Law—the use of biblical citations—was more apparent than real. Biblical citations on homicide in the New England codes supported rather than replaced English law. Earlier English commentators had gone almost as far as the Puritans in the use of the Bible; Coke, for example, also cited biblical authority for capital punishment of murder. As Fortescue and St. Germaine had before him, Coke added biblical citations to reinforce and make universal his legal arguments. In this convention, as in their other conformities to English law, Puritan lawmakers were English jurists, not innovators. The Bible explicitly punished infanticide with death, but the codemakers of New England did not mention the crime of infanticide, for they never derived their notions of homicide from holy scripture. The makers of law and triers of fact in New England viewed infanticide as a common law murder.[8]

The murder of an older child presented few legal problems in the New England courts. In these cases, Massachusetts and Plymouth courts acquitted 15 and convicted nine.

One acquittal and three convictions were handed down before 1670. The rate of conviction for defendants in later cases was two of four in the years between 1670 and 1699, one of five between 1700 and 1729, and three of 11 from 1730 to 1779. Two of the convictions in the period between 1730 and 1779 were of Indian and black slaves and servants for murdering the children of whites. In Connecticut, two of five cases of the murder of older children ended in convictions; in both, the mothers were found mentally incapable of controlling their actions, and were released after special verdicts.[9]

The pattern of treatment of bastard neonaticides is far more complex in both colonies and deserves closer attention. A graph comparing the conviction rate for all Massachusetts infanticide cases with those that would technically fall under the rule of the Stuart infanticide statute of 1624 shows a sharp break early in the eighteenth century. Prior to the 1730s, Massachusetts juries were convicting suspects of bastard neonaticide at a rate comparable to England after 1624: 17 of 31 cases ended in guilty verdicts. After 1730, only one of the 20 cases of bastard neonaticide ended in conviction. The three seventeenth-century Connecticut cases of this type resulted in one guilty verdict for murder, one guilty verdict for adultery, and one guilty verdict for neglect. Between 1700 and 1730, three of seven such cases there ended in conviction. Between 1730 and 1780, one of five Connecticut bastard neonaticide cases ended with conviction.

The rate of guilty verdicts in both New England colonies before 1730 is not surprising, given the severity of 21 James I, c. 27, but the truth is more complex. The statute itself was not permanently incorporated into the colonial laws of Massachusetts until 1696 (after a 1692 reception was disallowed by the privy council), nor in Connecticut until 1699. The conviction rate in Massachusetts from 1630 to 1696 for cases that would have fallen under the English law of 1624 was nine of 14, (64 percent), but after the statute was adopted, declined to seven of 33 (52 percent) by 1730, and

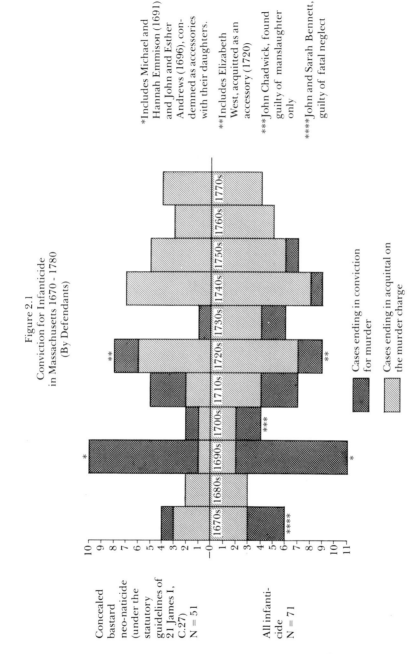

Figure 2.1
Conviction for Infanticide
in Massachusetts 1670 - 1780
(By Defendants)

*Includes Michael and
Hannah Emmison (1691)
and John and Esther
Andrews (1696), con-
demned as accessories
with their daughters.

**Includes Elizabeth
West, acquitted as an
accessory (1720)

***John Chadwick, found
guilty of manslaughter
only

****John and Sarah Bennett,
guilty of fatal neglect

Concealed
bastard
neo-naticide
(under the
statutory
guidelines of
21 James I,
C.27)
N = 51

All infanti-
cide
N = 71

Cases ending in conviction
for murder

Cases ending in acquittal on
the murder charge

fell to 19 of 53 (34 percent) by 1780. The sharp break in the initial pattern of conviction lies between 1720 and 1740. For the period between 1630 and 1730, the courts did not need the evidentiary guidance of the English infanticide statute to find unmarried women suspected of neonaticide guilty of murder. Uninstructed by statute, the conviction rate in New England before 1730 mirrored that in England. New England judges and trial juries had found ways to deal with concealed infant murder as severe as those in the Jacobean courts.[10]

Official accounts of the trials and punishments of the first infanticide offenders illustrate the initial responses of New England authorities to the crime. While the evidence might be different, the judges did not distinguish between neonaticide and the murder of older children by parents. Both caused concern; both were threats to the entire community. In 1638, Dorothy Talbie, of Salem, was tried and convicted for the murder of her daughter. Winthrop recorded the affair at length in his journal, marking it as an important event in the colony's brief history:

> [December 6.] Dorothy Talbye was hanged at Boston for murdering her own daughter, a child of three years old. She had been a member of the church of Salem, and of good esteem for godliness, etc; but, falling at difference with her husband, through melancholy or spiritual delusions, she sometimes attempted to kill him and her children, and herself, by refusing meat, saying it was so revealed to her, etc. After much patience, and divers admonitions not prevailing, the church cast her out. Whereupon she grew worse; so as the magistrate caused her to be whipped. Whereupon she was reformed for a time, and carried herself more dutifully to her husband, etc.; but soon after she was so possessed with Satan that he persuaded her (by his delusions, which she listened to as revelations from God) to break the neck of her own child, that she might free it from future misery. This she confessed upon her apprehension; yet, at the arraignment, she stood mute . . . till the governor told her she should be pressed to death, and then she confessed the indictment. When she was to receive judgment, she would not uncover

her face, nor stand up, but as she was forced, nor give any testimony of her repentance, either then or at her execution. The cloth, which should have covered her face, she plucked off and put between the rope and her neck. She desired to have been beheaded, giving this reason, that it was less painful and less shameful. After a swing or two, she catched at the ladder. Mr. Peter, her late pastor, and Mr. Wilson, went with her to the place of execution, but could do no good with her. Mr. Peter gave an exhortation to the people to take heed of revelations, etc., and of despising the ordinance of excommunication as she had done; for when it was to have been denounced against her, she turned her back, and would have gone forth, if she had not been stayed by force.[11]

Talbie's madness went unquestioned by Winthrop, yet she was not pardoned. Similar English cases went not to the noose, but ended in royal pardons on application of the assize justices to the crown. The manner in which Winthrop dwelt upon Talbie's prior history of offenses against the church suggests the reason for her execution. The facts that Winthrop gave were intended to prove that Talbie was guilty of something more than mere commission of a crime. Talbie had offended God, for she struck out against lay and clerical authority as well as her family. Her triers and judges believed that the devils she thought she saw were real indeed, and in confessing to her crime, she confessed to the sway that the powers of darkness had over all unwary Puritans.[12]

New England magistrates' concern for crimes like this was continuous, and their suspicions easily aroused. Talbie's case in the Bay Colony was preceded by a grand jury investigation of Mary Osborne for murdering her daughter. The jurors did not indict her. In 1642, Ann Hett was whipped for attempting to drown her child, whose age was not given in the indictment. Like Talbie, Hett had already been disciplined by her church for "scandalous speeches" against God on the sabbath, and for "unruliness" with her spouse. In 1648, Mary Allen of Lygonia, Maine, was named as the murderer of her child before the county court. She was prosecuted by Justice George Cleeve, but not indicted before the court of assistants. Puritan judges never underestimated the human potential for infant murder. In 1705, Justice Samuel Sewall warned his colleagues in the council against a law on miscegenation that might lead to "murders and other abominations" against the infant products of such mixed unions.[13]

Suspicion of attempted infanticide brought swift and severe chastisement in New England, and trials for the crime were major communal dramas. In 1648, Plymouth's magistrates provided elaborately for an inquest and trial in the death of Martha Clark, the four-year-old daughter of Allice Bishop. Allice was married to Richard Bishop, and evidently brought a child into the household, "the fruit of her own body." The girl was found with her throat cut in an upper room of the house. At an inquest held on July 22, 1648, Allice admitted her guilt, and said she was sorry. The general court of Plymouth, sitting in its judicial capacity, heard a grand jury of 17 men find a true bill in the case, and a trial jury of 12 pronounce Allice guilty. She was executed. The trouble the colony took to try her even after Bishop confessed to the crime, the indifference to what must have been her mental distress at its commission, and the great attention given to the details of the crime in the records, suggest that everyone in the government, from Governor Bradford to the court clerk, viewed Bishop's act with foreboding. The grisly facts of the infant's murder contributed to the solemnity of the trial, and the disruptive effect of Bishop's violence went far beyond her own domestic circle.[14]

As Bishop went to the gallows for murdering her four-year-old, Massachusetts' court of assistants judged Mary Martin for killing her newborn bastard. Again Winthrop was sufficiently moved and agitated by the case to include a full account of it in his journal:

> A merchant of Plymouth in England . . . came to Casco Bay, and after some time, having occasion to return into England, he left behind him two daughters, . . . but took not that

course for their safe bestowing in his absence, as the care and wisdom of a father should have done, so as the eldest of them, called Mary, twenty-one years of age, being in [the] house with one Mr. Mitton, a married man of Casco, within one quarter of a year, he was taken with her, and soliciting her chastity, obtained his desire, and having divers times committed sin with her, in the space of three months, she then moved to Boston, and put herself in service to Mrs. Bourne; and finding herself to be with child, and not able to bear the shame of it, she concealed it, and though divers did suspect it, and some told her mistress their fears, yet her behavior was so modest, and so faithful she was in her service, as her mistress would not give ear to any such report, but blamed such as told her of it. But, her time being come, she was delivered of a woman child in a back room by herself upon . . . [December 13, 1648] in the night, and the child was born alive, she kneeled upon the head of it till she thought it had been dead, and having laid it by, the child, being strong, recovered, and cried again. Then she took it again, and used violence to it till it was quite dead . . . a midwife in the town, having formerly suspected her, and now coming to her again, found she had been delivered of a child, which, upon examination she confessed, but said it was still-born, and so she put it into the fire. But, search being made, it was found in her chest, and when she was brought before the jury, they caused her to touch the face of it, whereupon the blood came fresh into it. Whereupon she confessed the whole truth, and a surgeon, being called to search the body of the child, found a fracture in the skull. Before she was condemned, she confessed, that she had prostituted her body to another also, one Sears. She behaved herself very penitently while she was in prison, and at her death. . . .

Massachusetts law did not incorporate the elaborate punishment for bastardy given in the English poor laws until 1660; it was Martin's modesty, not her fear of legal punishment, to which Winthrop attributed her conduct. Unlike Talbie, Martin had professed her contrition in addition to her guilt. This made her case "sad" for Winthrop, but he persisted in relating her death throes. The community participated cathartically in her expiation of sin.[15]

Official concern for infanticide, joined to juries' willingness to convict suspects, argues the urgency which authority and laity assigned to prosecution of this crime. From the earliest cases through the first decades of the eighteenth century, a harsh message issued forth. Those found guilty of the murder of infants in Massachusetts before 1730 were executed, not pardoned. The message predated Massachusetts and Connecticut laws against bastardy, and cannot therefore be mere repetition of the developments traced in Chapter 1. The conviction rate in England was slightly higher than that in New England, but the former was under the prodding of 21 James I, c. 27. What is more, Massachusetts had higher indictment rates than metropolitan London for this crime (see Appendix 4). Puritans in the mother country had played an important part in the passage of the infanticide law; perhaps its tenets were so thoroughly woven into the fabric of their own views on crime and punishment that they did not need to pass it in their own communities.[16]

Even if this were so, one must ask and answer the question why Puritans in Massachusetts and Connecticut considered infanticide accusations so dangerous to society? A number of plausible hypotheses prove untenable upon closer examination. High conviction rates did not result from the general severity of New England courts, nor from a special affection for children in New England, nor from Puritan magistrates' attempts to enforce class distinctions, nor from the harshness of biblical codes of laws.

The message of the concern of judges over infancticide and the high conviction rate was not merely a horror of all interpersonal violence, or the fear of its potential increase if unchecked. Violent death did not shock judges into severe reprisals. In Massachusetts, the conviction rate for the murder of adults over the period from 1630 to 1692 was 40 percent (18 of 45)—notably lower than for infanticide. Although manslaughter was a capital offense mentioned in the *Body of Liberties*—unlike infanticide—only one conviction for it led to death. Between 1673 and 1683, seven convictions for manslaughter resulted in whippings and other penalties; none in hanging. Nor did the volume of infanticide drive juries to guilty verdicts. Although the calculation of crime rates from indictments are as speculative in New England as in Old England, comparably computed indictment rates for different jurisdictions may still reveal trends. The incidence of infanticide in seventeenth-century Massachusetts was 1.58 per hundred thousand people, per year, while that for Maryland was 5.65 per hundred thousand. The Maryland statistic is, if anything, too low, for estimates of the population there are steadily being reduced by scholars. Nevertheless, despite a higher indictment rate for infanticide, the Maryland conviction rate was far lower than that of Massachusetts. In Maryland, between 1656 and 1676, only five of 14 suspects indicted for neonaticide were found guilty. In addition, the Stuart infanticide law might have been cited in Maryland cases, as in Joan Colledge's case (1673), when the proprietor's prosecutor demanded she be convicted "for a murder in concealing the birth of the child." If it were received, the infanticide statute of 1624 should have led to a higher conviction rate in the Calverts' domain than in New England, but it did not.[17]

Connecticut followed Massachusetts. The Connecticut courts sentenced convicted married defendants more leniently than Bay Colony courts, but overall neonaticide conviction rates in Connecticut and Massachusetts were very similar. Mercy Brown and Katherine Wyar were found guilty of the murder of their older infants, although juries in the 1691 and 1709 cases ordered the two women placed in the custody of their families when they were found to be insane. Ruth Briggs was convicted of a bastard neonaticide in 1668 and probably executed. Hannah Hackleton was acquitted of the crime in 1665 but convicted of illicit sexual behavior. The only other neonaticide in early Connecticut was Amy Munn's case, discussed later in this chapter.[18]

Nor was the message of the high neonaticide conviction

rate between 1630 and 1730 to love and cherish children above all else. In New England, fatal infant abuse cases in which parents or caretakers were suspected of permitting infants or young servants to die of neglect or from beatings, resulted in only one conviction for murder. William Frankling of Boston was executed in 1643 for beating his servant boy to death. For similar acts, Robert Latham of Plymouth was only burned in the hand (as though it were a manslaughter) and fined. Winthrop reported the acquittal of Marmaduke Perry, of Salem, in 1639, for a fatal beating of his apprentice, when the trial jury could not agree on a verdict. In 1674, John and Sarah Bennett were acquitted of murder in the fatal neglect of a girl left with them. They had only to pay fines and costs. John Chadwick was found not guilty of the murder of his 14-month-old son, but was punished for the manslaughter at the superior court in 1712. This followed the English pattern, where the right to discipline children and servants went almost unquestioned. Behind the willingness to punish children lay the sanction of traditional disengagement between parents and small children. Some New England families may have been exceptions to the rule, but for many children life was brutal, nasty, and short. Epidemics of smallpox killed off almost one-fifth of Boston's population in 1677 and 1678, and the children suffered the worst. "The presence of early death everywhere" did not make life more precious, but instead cautioned against holding a child's life too dear.[19]

Punishment of a crime like infanticide may indirectly enforce social and economic class distinctions. Capital punishment can be an effective social control mechanism. Among the characteristics of infanticide defendants, servitude, with its potential for social disobedience, unmarried pregnancy, with its implied defiance of domesticity, and ethnic differences, in an era of intense English ethnocentrism, might have induced juries to look beyond the crime to the security of the community as they rendered their decisions. If the unwed mother, the servant mother, or the mother from an ethnic minority was seen to threaten social order and discipline, a jury might lean toward a guilty verdict despite weak evidence in the case. In this fashion a "dangerous class" of women would become the target of bias in the courts.[20]

A test for this is available: cross-tabulating acquittals and convictions with servitude, marital status, and ethnicity among the suspects. For defendants and accessories, between 1638 and 1730, on whom the information was available, one finds four of 11 of the guilty were servants, while five of 13 among the not guilty were bound for service. Ten of 20 defendants found guilty were married while nine of 21 found not guilty were married. The ratios do not show enough divergence to support the hypothesis that mere servitude or spinsterhood had prejudiced jurors. Of course, jurors probably took some note of the marital status and social position of a defendant. A well-to-do wife lacked a motive for infanticide, and might have powerful friends. At Sarah Moore's trial in Connecticut in 1702 for the crime of neonaticide:

> The jury found a verdict of not guilty. The jury was sympathetic to an implausible story (unless the woman was retarded which is never mentioned). But, the husband, Joseph Moore, was the son of one of the highest status individuals in town. His father was not a member of the provincial elite, but he was a selectman and quite well-to-do as his son became upon assuming his property.

A prominent family did not always guarantee acquittal— Sarah Threeneedles, spinster daughter of well-respected parents, was executed for infanticide in 1698—but combined with marriage, good family was a potent defense against these charges.[21]

There is one tantalizing exception to this set of conclusions on social control: race. Racial prejudice, social tension, or a jury's consensus that black servants and slaves had good reason to avoid the stigma and burdens of bastardy, might be present in the trials of blacks for infanticide. For the entire 1670 to 1780 period, blacks were found guilty of the crime at one and a half times the rate of whites, in five of 11 cases. While blacks constituted no more than 3 or 4 percent of the population in New England, they numbered 11 (15 percent) of the defendants in Massachusetts from 1670 to 1780. This disproportion of black cases might have reflected their despair or anger, or a selective application of the laws against them. In contrast, only one of the five Indians indicted for six infanticides between 1630 and 1780 was found guilty. This was Patience, a servant accused of murdering an eight-year-old white boy in 1735. (Patience, an Indian woman, was actually tried twice in the 1730's for infanticide. Acquitted on the charge of murdering her own newborn bastard, she was later convicted for strangling her master's neighbor's young son and throwing the body into a well.) Indians charged with murder of Indian children were acquitted. Indians, like blacks, were considered racially inferior in the colony, but by the 1690s Indians living within the settled portions of the New England colonies posed little threat to social harmony. At the same time, unlike the black slave, Indians were not a ready source of labor nor potential breeders of negotiable property. Also, the Indians among the colonists were not so closely watched as the blacks, making it more difficult to find witnesses and evidence against the former.[22]

Finally, the high conviction rate was not determined by the solemn Mosaic aura of the criminal code. It is true that an atmosphere of sin and redemption hung over the assistants assembled as a court, but other mortal crimes tried there under the codes did not have a comparable percentage of guilty verdicts. More important, the pattern of verdicts in infanticide cases continued into the decades after the arrival of the new charter of 1691 and the replacement of biblical citations and codes with English procedural and substantive law. Of the cases fitting the Stuart infanticide law in the three decades after the demise of the codes, eight of 17 resulted in convictions, but three of the acquittals came near the end of the 1720s. In some respects, the codes should have mitigated prosecution for infanticide. The codes did not mention infanticide specifically, or adopt the infanticide statute of 1624. In addition, the codes provided that two witnesses were to testify in every capital trial. In infanticide cases such witnesses most often could do little more than recite the circumstances of the discovery of the victim or the prior concealment of pregnancy by the unwed suspect. The Jacobean infanticide law gave far more weight to such witnesses than the New England codes, while limiting friendly testimony to those who could establish the death of the infant during or before delivery.[23]

In fact, eyewitness testimony was not as important in these trials as certain kinds of circumstances, which an entire community, acting through it magistrates, could judge. This was the circumstantial evidence that Winthrop had emphasized in his journals: first the concealment of sin, second, prior sexual wantoness, and third, the disobedience of women to community standards. In such evidence lay corroboration of the magistrates' suspicions of the corruptibility of the defendant. Her reputation and their presumptions about the connections between concealment and sexual immorality, almost as much as proof of commission of the crime, led to conviction. While not ignoring common law criminal precepts about murder, infanticide verdicts in New England showed the force of these three larger ruling Puritan conceptions of sin.

The first of these ruling precepts was that concealment of sin violated God's law and man's law. Concealment denied personal readiness for salvation. A fear of concealment of sin within the corrupt body of the English church had led to the first organized Puritan protests in England. Michael Wigglesworth, Harvard tutor, minister, and poet to the generation of founders, wrestled with this danger in his didactic poem, "Day of Doom." He admonished his readers that there would be no concealment on the day of judgment. God would tear off all cloaks from the soul's hidden sins. Secret sin, abominations of the flesh, and hardness of the spirit warned the Puritan of his ultimate destruction. The act of hiding sin from God was a proof of an unregenerate

heart. In 1672, Reverend Thomas Shepard offered serious
advice to his son, then about to enter Harvard College: "Remember now to be watchful against the two great Sins of
many Scholars; the first is youthful Lusts, speculative wantonness, and secret filthiness, which God sees in the Dark,
and for which God hardens and blinds young men's hearts
. . . The second is malignancy and secret distaste of Holi-
ness and the Power of Godliness . . ." The community of
saints guided, encouraged, and stood ready to aid its members in confessing and remedying transgressions. Refusal to
avow errors to one's fellow Puritans was as much a sin as
refusal to admit them to oneself. The covenanted community could not withstand concealed evil within itself and remain pure. Upon this theological premise was constructed
the intrusive network of Puritan privacy laws. "Prying
neighbors and active magistrates ferreted out these [morals]
offenses and prosecuted them" for the hidden sin was the
downfall of all.[24]

Puritan thought assigned heightened meaning to the conventional English form of indictment for capital crimes
"without having God before her eyes, and instigated by the
Devil." Wigglesworth anguished that "the Lord hides away
his face which is all that I have in the land of the Living."
The indictment itself contained a theological judgment
upon the criminal—she was a concealer of sin. Even the victim who concealed a crime was thought to be guilty of an
affront to God, church, and community, as indicated by the
New Haven magistrates who punished a married couple for
not reporting an attempted rape upon the wife. Disclosure
by the offender might bring a lessening of penalties, as it
regularly did for fornicators in Connecticut's particular
court and in the county courts of Massachusetts. The persistent efforts of judges and ministers to obtain and publish
confessions and repentances of the guilty as they stood
upon the gallows grew in part from the belief that crimes
must not be hidden, even by those about to die.[25]

Judges' aversion to the concealment of sin in infanticide
cases is apparent in the examinations of Elizabeth Emmison

in 1691, and Sarah Smith, in 1698. The interrogations of the two women, separated by seven years, read as though the magistrates had a prepared form in their hands. "Why did you not call for help" they asked, in a ritual, almost catechismic pattern of question and answer. Why was birth concealed? Why was no preparation for delivery made? Why was the death (which the defendants claimed was due to natural causes) not brought to the attention of others? The jury was being told, as it heard these examinations, that the crime lay not only in the murder, but in the concealment surrounding it. The rigor and length of these examinations, and their stress upon concealment, went beyond otherwise comparable investigations in other colonies. In June, 1715, for example, Mary Richardson was questioned about the suspicious death of her newborn bastard by Richmond County, Virginia, justices. Only once did the justices ask why she had not cried her help. Her answer, "I was a fool, and knew no better" may or may not have satisfied them, but they did not pursue the matter. Instead, they pressed on to the question of paternity. There was nothing catechismic in their approach. Of course, Emmison's and Smith's denials were not believed in part because they had admitted to having previous illicit sexual experience. This made them immoral women as well as suspected murderesses.[26]

The second underlying precept of the law concerning infanticide was its hostility to sexual irregularities. Against these, the Puritans in England contributed to a flood of legislation controlling sexual conduct. From the pulpit, Puritan ministers in England had thundered against the uncleanness of the wanton. The sins of the flesh were many, and the good Puritan, while not abandoning the world, was expected to shun these temptations. In Massachusetts, poet Anne Bradstreet held these sins at bay in her dialogue between "The Flesh and the Spirit": "Be still thou unregenerate part,/Disturb no more my settled heart,/For I have vowed (and so will doe)/ Thee as a foe, still, to pursue,/And combate with thee will and must." New World Puritan pen alties for fornication, wanton dalliance, and a host of other sexual miscarriages, were severe, and the vast majority of those accused were convicted and punished. Adultery, which struck at family life as well as sexual restraint, was but a misdemeanor in England, but Massachusetts and Connecticut codes made it a capital offense. The Plymouth colony did not go this far, but it still condemned adultery rigorously in its criminal laws.[27]

These colonies' court records are filled with sex offenses. The early population of Massachusetts and its neighbors is too small to attempt to compute crime rates, but the records show concern with these crimes. Even on the wilderness fringes of the Bay Colony, sex crimes were prosecuted. In Saco, Maine, Mary Puddington's 1640 case involved magistrates, family, neighbors, and the town minister. Mary was the wife of George Puddington of Agamenticus, but was known to frequent "the house and company" of the town's minister, George Burdette. She also abused her husband "to the great scandal and disturbance of the said plantation." Mary was induced to atone publicly for her "light carriage," and beg the forgiveness of her husband on her knees. Burdette, "a man of ill name and fame, infamous for incontinency, a Publisher and Broacher of diverse dangerous speeches, the better to seduce that weak sex of woman to his incontinent practices . . ." was fined 30 pounds sterling for his misconduct with Puddington and other women. To the south, in New Haven, civil authorities regularly whipped offenders for "base carriage and filthy dalliance" in these years. From July 1642 to the following June, the New Haven magistrates heard and ordered corporal punishment in five cases of fornication and wanton dalliance. From 1640 to 1643, the Connecticut particular court rendered judgment in five cases of sexual abuses, and in the same years more populous Massachusetts Bay was beset with two cases of fornication, five cases of lewd behavior and seduction, and two ravishments, the last of which ended with the whipping of two boys. On July 7, 1641, both partners in an adulterous union were whipped, the court choosing to treat their actions not as adultery, but "filthy carriage." In the years 1634 to 1644, 20 cases of lewd behavior, 16 of fornication, and four of adultery (three with charges reduced to a lesser offense), required the Massachusetts assistants' attention. All but two of these morals cases ended with some form of public punishment. In the later portions of the seventeenth century, county courts were inundated with these cases. Between 1671 and 1674, county courts in Essex and Suffolk, Massachusetts, judged 94 cases of fornication and 33 cases of lewd behavior. The sheer number of sexual irregularity cases reported by neighbors to magistrates, and the willingness of magistrates to pursue offenders—all these county cases ended in some penalty—meant that the criminal justice system took these offenses seriously. Every inhabitant was expected to live up to the high standards of the law. Masters stood with servants and old residents with newcomers in the dock. But overwhelmingly the young, the unmarried, and the servant bore the brunt of suspicion and conviction for sexual offenses. In this last context, post-1660 laws punishing the poor mothers and fathers of bastards—young servants of both sexes—linked infanticide to incontinence.[28]

Evidence of illegitimacy, as in Emmison's case, or of prior fornication, as in Emmison's and Martin's cases, or of adultery, as in Smith's case, weighted the evidentiary scales against defendants in infanticide trials. Wantonness corrupted the soul, while concealment of wantonness prevented due contrition. The progress from sin to sin was thought to be inevitable, leading from fornication to bastardy and finally infanticide. As in England, the colonial law on bastardy gave an incentive for the crimes. Cross-tabulation of the legitimacy of the victims with the concealment of their corpses shows a very strong and statistically significant association between illegitimacy and concealment.

Statistical analysis of these cases confirms a fact that must have been apparent to judges and juries: The single mother concealed the corpse of her own suspiciously dead child, while married women did not conceal the deaths of their children nearly so often—though these might be suspicious, or display signs of violent assault. (A cross-tabulation of the 33 defendants between 1638 and 1730 on whose cases the relevant data was found, shows phi = .620, with significance at the 99 percent level.) A second cross-tabulation, of legitimacy and victim age, shows an equally strong association between the legitimacy of the victim and the age at which it was supposedly murdered. The legitimate child risked murder with about equal probability throughout its young life. The illegitimate child faced the most acute risk of murder before it had reached the end of its first day. The threat of the latter fate was considerable, far greater than the threat to the legitimate baby. After the first day of life, the bastard child for all intents and purposes faced little danger of murder from its caretakers. The fact that fewer bastards were murdered after the first 24 hours of life than legitimate children may be due to the large number of bastard neonaticides in comparison to the small number of legitimate victims of neonaticide. The strength and significance of the relationship between the age of the victim and the legitimacy of the victim is presented in Table 2.1. This connection among illegitimacy, concealment, and the age of the victim could not have escaped the attention of magistrates already concerned with concealment of sexual immorality.

The third of the underlying precepts beneath the high conviction rate for bastard neonaticide concerned the gender of the suspects. Women were weak; they concealed sin and undermined public morals and order. In England and New England the campaign against the evil woman exploded in the prosecution of witchcraft. Witching—causing harm through magic, or divination, or any form of sorcery—was as much a woman's crime in New England as it was in the mother country. After reading documentary accounts of witchcraft trials, psychiatrist Wolfgang Lederer wrote "the main feeling vented with regard to witchcraft was that of fear of women and hate of women." John Demos has revealed the rich, complex combination of projection and displacement against older women at work in the

Table 2.1
Illegitimacy by Age of the Victim, Massachusetts Infanticide, 1630–1730 [a]

Was the victim legitimate?	Age of the Victim			
	Neonate	*Under Two*	*Under Nine*	
Yes				
Actual count	2	3	1	6
Row percentage	33.3	50.0	16.7	16.2%
Column percentage	6.5	75.0	50.0	
Total percentage	5.4	8.1	2.7	
No				
Actual count	29	1	1	31
Row percentage	93.5	3.2	3.2	83.8%
Column percentage	93.5	25.0	50.0	
Total percentage	78.4	2.7	2.7	N =
	31	4	2	37
	83.8%	10.8%	5.4%	100.0%

[a] Cramer's $V = .616$; significant at the 99 percent level.

accusation and trial of witches in New England. As already seen, witchcraft and the murder of children are closely related crimes. The Salem, Massachusetts witches, overwhelmingly older women, some of whom clearly stood at the edge of society, were suspected of raining their shafts upon children. Still clearer cases of witches' "maleficium" against the very young can be found in the colonial record. In 1651, Mary Parsons was tried by a Boston jury for the bewitchment of her one-year-old son, Joshua. In 1680, Hampton Goodwife Rachel Fuller was convicted of infanticide by witchcraft. Eight years later, an Irish widow, Goodwife Glover, was executed in Boston for bewitching her four children. Such accusations are not in the same class as infanticide cases because no grounds exist to believe that infanticide could result from such proximate causes. In addition, bewitching of children must not be classed with infanticide cases lest the two caterories contaminate each other statistically. One nevertheless cannot ignore clues like the fact that Elizabeth Emmison's family had fallen afoul of the Salem witchcraft inquisitors, perhaps impeaching the entire clan in the eyes of the jury. As in many witchcraft cases, Andrews' and Emmison's parents were indicted as accessories. Witchcraft threatened society with a ferocious form of female deviance. For jurors and judges, infanticide might have had the same dark power.[29]

One way of testing the thesis which states that beneath the conviction rate for infanticide lay the same fear of women that stimulated the witchcraft mania, is to compare the periodicity of the conviction rates for the two crimes. For all the accusations that neighbors made against each other, very few women were convicted and executed for witchcraft in New England until the 1690s. Only three were actually condemned to death in Massachusetts before the Salem trials. In the 1690s this changed. Of the first 12 men and women tried by the special court of oyer and terminer sitting at Salem in 1692, all were convicted and 11 were executed. The sheer magnitude of the episode bespeaks not only a local crisis, but a trauma spread across the face of the colony. Massachusetts' leading jurists sat upon the bench, and its leading ministers offered their advice as the trials unfolded. Over a similar course of time, convictions for infanticide followed the pattern in Figure 2.2. The striking jump in convictions in the 1690s is suggestive, if one assumes that, as in England, the volume of witchcraft accusations and the volume of infanticide reports were influenced by the same fear of disorder, reflecting and exacerbated by real social and economic disruption. Surely these fears were abroad in the Bay Colony in the 1690s, as the Puritan mission seemed threatened from within and without, and the Puritans' leaders faced the loss of control of their own experiment in the wilderness.[30]

All of these underlying themes came together in sermons given at infanticide executions. On the eve of the hanging of women for the murder of their children, well attended public lectures permitted the community to share in her agony and learn from her fate. Puritan ministers reminded their flocks of the principles behind capital punishment of

Figure 2.2
Indictments and Convictions
for Infanticide in
Seventeenth-century Massachusetts

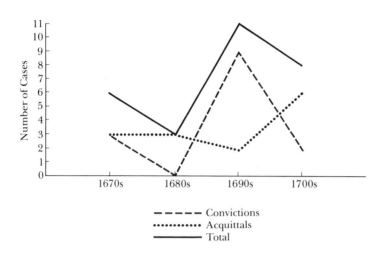

sinful women. Cotton Mather was a practiced and popular authority on the criminality of women. Early in the 1690s, he had urged the scourging of the Salem witches. He proudly noted in his diary on November 17, 1698, that he had to climb over and around the bodies of thousands come to hear him preach before the execution of Sarah Three-needles, condemned for infanticide. In his *Pillars of Salt, an History of Some Criminals Executed in This Land for Capital Crimes* (1699), Mather expanded upon his sermons on the execution of Threeneedles and Sarah Smith to discourse upon other murdering mothers. The "uncleanness" and concealment of sin were his first targets. All sin was debauchery and sign of an "unclean" spirit. Wantonness lay in every man and woman's "secret heart," for the more people sinned, the more they strove to hide their sins. His first example was the temptress of David, Bathsheba, and his last was Sarah Smith. For these women and their paramours, "the fire of lust" became "the fire of hell." In keeping with his choice of theme, the majority of the capital offenses narrated by Mather were neonaticides involving concealment, sexual immorality, and female disobedience of authority. From his discussion of Mary Martin's 1648 murder of her baby to the Sarah Smith execution, Mather hammered at the uncleanness, the concealment, and the disregard of authority in infanticide cases. Admonitions to the young against the external dangers of such conduct concluded Mather's essay. In Deerfield, where Smith met her fate, Reverend John Williams also preached on her execution day. He coupled murder with uncleanness and cited Smith's admission of previous adulteries. All "whore mongers," he warned, lay under a sentence of eternal death. The "secret sins" of "hardened women" like Smith would be proclaimed before all the world at the day of judgment or before the entire colony, if discovered sooner. All of this augury was directed to women, the worst of whom were "mothers of bastards," fornicators, adulteresses, "witches," and "whores." Williams, like Mather, closed with a warning to a "wicked generation" not to fall into Smith's snare.[31]

A moving last echo of this genre was Thomas Foxcroft's *Lessons of Caution for Young Sinners.* It was preached at the ultimate colonial Massachusetts execution of an unmarried woman for infanticide. Rebecca Chamblit of Boston was convicted in August 1733, under the strict guidelines of the 1696 act, for the murder of her male neonate. Unlike Smith and Emmison, she was not evasive or hardened. With minister Mather Byles, she prayed for her own salvation in the days between conviction and execution. Byles recorded her responses to his questions on the way to the gallows. Even though the ritual trappings of the entire episode reduced her to a minor role in a socio-religious drama, her replies retain their affecting quality. "Oh, I'm afraid, I'm afraid" she cried out, but under Byles' guidance she reaffirmed her hope for grace. He told her to prepare herself, a common and orthodox Puritan lesson even for the most virtuous. Foxcroft's sermon opened with a commendation of Chamblit for allowing herself and her deeds to be used to warn others of her fate. Through him, she testified that "the mask is pulled off, or thrown off" unclean youth. The carnal life became the criminal life. Foxcroft's closing plea against "philosophy and vain decit after the wisdom of this world" was a final appeal to an older Puritan faith against secular, immodest modernity.[32]

With the three underlying concerns of seventeenth-century Puritan judges and juries in mind, the reception of the English infanticide law in New England falls into proper perspective. The colonial version of the 1624 Jacobean statute was not needed as a rule of evidence, for the prosecution gained convictions on proof of concealment and prior sexual irregularity without it. Instead, the incorporation of the statute, first in 1692, and again in 1696, provided a formal clarification and restatement of Puritan criminal precepts in Anglicized terms at a time when Puritan courts and codes were giving way to English jurisprudence. The precise timing of reception was itself due to a series of complex neonaticide trials.

The infanticide law was received in Massachusetts in 1692, after one notorious case of newborn bastard infanticide, and revived in 1696, after a second case. The first concerned Elizabeth Emmison and her parents. On May 10, 1691, a jury of inquest found that Emmison, of Haverhill, the unwed daughter of Michael and Hannah Emmison, had given birth to twins in her father's house, and murdered them. She concealed the bodies in a cloth bag, which she buried in her father's yard. In her testimony before the inquest, she admitted that on seven occasions she had slept with Samuel Lad, one of which trysts had resulted in the twins. She was also suspected of bearing and losing a bastard child previously. In her defense, she claimed the twins were born dead, and while everyone was at church she took them from the closet where she had hidden them and buried them behind her father's house. Her father and mother were examined as well. They testified that they knew nothing of their daughter's travail. Although the corpses were sewn in a cloth, Hannah Emmison denied assisting her daughter in the concealment of the crime. No evidence of violence to the twins was presented, but they appeared to be full term. The transcript of Emmison's testimony shows that the daughter based her defense upon the stillbirth of the children. Only circumstantial evidence—the fact of concealment, and her refusal to reveal her condition—could be used against her. The jury found the evidence sufficient to convict. Her parents' denials were suspect, for in Elizabeth's condition, it would have been a feat for her to conceal the pregnancy and the births, and then arrange the burial on her parents' property without help from them. All three were impeached as witnesses, sentenced to death, and two years later Elizabeth was executed.[33]

The second case involved Susanah Andrews of Plymouth, who in March 1696 was found guilty of murdering her twins, again with the assistance of her parents. Her parents were convicted as accessories and also sentenced to death. The likelihood of a conspiracy to conceal the act had convinced a jury that a murder had occurred, for the planning that went into disposal of the victims implied premeditated effort. Without the guidance of the infanticide law, juries reached a guilty verdict for Andrewses.[34]

Andrews' case, reiterating the evidentiary issues in Emmison's case, and concluding with three execution orders, might have raised some anxiety about these proceedings within the colony. This was a worrisome time for Puritan courts in New England. The Massachusetts general court's first efforts to rewrite the capital laws and refashion the superior court had been rejected in England. Fearful that capital verdicts in the superior court reached in accord with their old standards of evidence might not be well received by the king's privy council and hopeful that the reading of the English infanticide statute to juries would avert this event, Puritan authorities bolstered themselves with the statute. The latter did not revise the rule of evidence then in use; it merely protected judge and jury as they applied established guidelines. Plymouth maiden Sarah Howland, the daughter of Joseph and Elizabeth Howland, was accused of murdering her bastard infant at the March 1699 session of the superior court, but the parents testified, as the statute permitted, that the child had been born dead, and Howland was acquitted. It is possible that the statute helped the entire family and would even have assisted the Emmisons and the Andrewes. More was probably involved in the juries' deliberations; perhaps the women's reputations were influential. Whatever rules of evidence were laid down by statute, jurors were the ultimate arbiters of the facts, and jurors chose to believe the Howlands' and not the others.[35]

In the same year that Sarah Howland was acquitted in Plymouth, the Connecticut court of assistants heard the case of Amy Munn. In May 1699, she pleaded not guilty to the charge of murder of her newborn bastard. The prosecutor's notes for summation of the case to the jury are preserved, a document rarely found in the records. The notes offer a clear perspective of the prosecution's use of evidence:

> May it please this Honobl. Court and Gent. of the Jury [.] In order to the prosecution of the Inditement drawen and charged against the Prisoner at the Bar [,] I offer the ensueing Evidences to prove her guilty of that malitious, fellonious, inhuman . . . cruelty of murthering a man child the conception and production of her own body. Imp. It was her premeditated resolve to make away this child before such time as she fell into the paines of travale . . . before she came to Farmington, test[imonie]s [of] Ann Wadsworth and Margaret Higginson.2nd She offered violence to the child in the Birth or bringing it forth into the world; see her acknowledgment before the Grand Jury. 1st. That she was afraid she had hurt the child in the Birth and by pulling the child she had broke the skin. See her confession before the Grand Jury: Test Matthew Allyn [,] John Hale. 2nd: In pursueance of her resolution to make away the child, she neglected all meanes and helps for preserveing the life of the child [,] would not cal[l] for any help though it was neer. 3rd She cast the Child into a corner of the room that her barbarous cruelty might not be discovered so that her designe and contrivance was to make away the Child and to conceale her murtherous intent [;] how effected [:] For by her confession before the Grand Jury the child was neer born when Mr. Wadsworth was in the room

with her[,] then she desired him go out of the room that she might effect her cruelty in destroying the child as the sequel manifests. 4 At the first discovery of the child it was found in the place where the prisoner at the Barr confessed she laid it at[,] at the corner of the room mortally wounded[,] the throat of it cut by some hand with a sharp edged instrument which would complete what she had before contrived which was not so fully effected by the violence that was offered unto the Child when she pulled it—So by her own confession that she thought the skin of the Child was broken: See the Returne of the Jury of Inquest[,] with her confession to the Grand Jury[.] And to add to her wickedness she endeavoured to make accessaries to this Horrible crime perswadeing Mr. Wadsworth and his wife to conceale this murther, so that by what is presented both by her own confession and by the several Testimonies it unavoidably centers upon the prisoner Amy Munn that she cruelly and felloniously murthered her own Child and is guilty as charged in the Inditement.[36]

Despite this summation, Munn was found guilty only of fornication and willful neglect of her child. The problem for the Connecticut court of assistants was the same posed by the Emmison and Andrews cases in Massachusetts. Concealment may or may not have been evidence of premeditation. The prosecutor tried to sway the jury in this direction, particularly with his reference to an earlier abortion attempt. The Wadsworths, her master and mistress, probably aided her in substantiating the reasonable defense that she concealed a stillborn or accidentially dead infant to preserve her reputation. The general assembly responded to the case with the adoption of the English statute. Like their counterparts in Massachusetts, the Connecticut lawmakers enacted the 1624 law verbatim.[37]

It is true that it would not have been necessary to consider receiving the Jacobean infanticide law in 1692, 1696, or 1699, had not English law begun to make its weight felt in the New England colonies. This process of Anglicization of the courts and of pleading was all but irresistible. Nothing in the new Massachusetts charter or the revision of the laws in New England demanded incorporation of the infanticide statute, however, and Rhode Island never did enact the 1624 law. The reason may have been simply the fact that its courts heard few cases of this type. It is possible that Massachusetts and Connecticut, like Virginia in 1710, received the statute because the governors and king's attorneys sought clarification of the law before seeking pardons from the king for convicted defendants. In point of fact, New England judges found methods of mitigating sentence without appeals to the king in council. Given the particular sequence of cases which preceded the reception, it appears more likely that the statute was adopted to remind juries of the presumptive guilt of murder which the concealment of bastardly entailed, and to restate, in terms consistent with the laws of the English realm, the special Puritan aversion to the concealed products of female "uncleanness."

With or without the English statute, into the 1720s powerful communal understandings about the nature of the crime of infanticide had guided judges and jurors in appraising evidence. After the 1720s, the pattern of convictions changed in the colony. The reception of the statute had little impact at a time when convictions were already common, and, conversely, had little effect after 1730, when the century-old pattern of conviction was transformed. After 1730, only four of the 30 indicted for infanticide in Massachusetts were convicted of the crime. In cases fitting the acts of 1692 and 1696, only one of 20 was found guilty. In the majority of the latter cases, the indictment noted the fact that the statute was read to the jury. If in New England, as in the mother country, conviction rates resulted from a mixture of official condemnation of the concealment of female sexual misconduct and the facts of particular cases, it seems plain that attitudes toward the crimes must have undergone a deep change in the decades after 1730.

Emblematic of these changing attitudes, the end of the 1720s saw the passing of the last of the generation of the Jeremiads. Cotton Mather died in 1728, a few years after his father, Increase. They had been defenders of the Puritan campaign against women's crimes and mortal enemies

of wanton female disobedience. With them, as Robert Middlekauff suggests, passed an epoch. In his last months,
"after years of begging his people to change their sinful
hearts, Cotton Mather admitted that New England should
not be confused with the New Jerusalem." A new generation of men sat in judgment of accused infanticide mothers.
One is left to conjecture whether the decline in the conviction rate was solely a reflection of the passing of Puritanism.
Or did the new leniency of New England courts reflect a
relaxation of punishment for infanticide in the mother
country, whose values the first Puritans had brought with
them? And if this were true, what were the common forces
behind this last step in the growth of modern infanticide
law?[38]

3

Reform,
England and New England, 1700-1803

Eighteenth-century England and New England witnessed a decline in the rates of the indictments for infanticide and the percentages of convictions as steep as their increases were in the Tudor and Jacobean era. (Throughout this chapter we move freely from England to New England, omitting repetitive and awkward qualifications because the decline in cases and convictions in the two places were parallel, if not equal, in size. There were some differences in the distribution of characteristics among defendants and victims, as well as in the absolute values of the rates of indictment in the two jurisdictions. These are discussed in Appendix 4 and Chapter 4.) Behind the turnabout in numbers in both England and New England lay numerous influences, ranging from the confines of courthouses to the broadest patterns of social life. Magistrates and officials prosecuted fewer women for the crime, and juries grew unwilling to condemn suspects, especially upon mere proof of concealment of birth. Successful defenses against the Jacobean infanticide statute emerged, and judges gave merciful rulings on evidence of stillbirth. Outside of the courtroom, society was growing more solicitous of mothers and more attentive to maternal sentiment. By the end of the century, statutory law came to reflect the changed atmosphere at the trials. Reform of the law followed the dictates of judicial experience and social norms just as, two centuries before, severe legislation on infanticide had codified sterner magisterial and community standards.

The effect of these reforming impulses was great but gradual. In the beginning of the eighteenth century, infanticide trials still bore the familiar character of the previous century. Even as New England adopted the English statute on infanticide to justify punishing the concealers of bastard infant death, observers in the mother country were bewailing the numbers of infanticides which even the severity of 21 James I, c. 27 could not deter. "Monsters," "barbarous" "merciless" "whores," Addison, Defoe, and their educated countrymen agreed, were doing away with their own children at a frightening pace. With brutal irony, Swift proclaimed that officials in Ireland had only to make the practice legal, and the food shortages there would disappear. These mournful voices notwithstanding, infanticide in England was not reaching epidemic proportions. Sensitive men might now be more aware of the enormity of the crime, but judges and juries were trying fewer and fewer cases proportional to the rise in population, and were resorting to the noose less frequently than they had in the previous century. An informative documentary survival of the highest courts of Middlesex and of the City of London, the *Old Bailey Sessions Papers,* allows detailed examination of these realities.[1]

The *Old Bailey Sessions Papers* (*OBSP*) were summary and later stenographic eyewitness reports of trials before the courts of general gaol delivery and oyer and terminer for the county of Middlesex and the City of London. From the mid-1670s through the end of the eighteenth century, these documents covered indictments and trials for infanticide in greater London and the surrounding countryside. Changing in style from chapbook to transcript, and in volume from a scattered few for the seventeenth century to an almost complete series for the later eighteenth century, the *OBSP* afford a perspective on the administration of criminal justice in the metropolis of the realm. While procedure cannot be discerned with clarity in the earliest *OBSP*, the treatment of infanticide cases seems familiar. All the attitudes encountered in earlier prosecution of the crime and the criminal, added to the devastating effect of the infanticide statute of 1624, are present in a typical 1679 case:

> The most considerable Tryal this Wednesday forenoon, was of a Woman for Murthering her Bastard Child; a Crime in it self so horrid and unnatural, as one would think no person, especially of that Sex, which is counted the most tender-hearted and merciful, could be guilty of such an inhumane Impiety, and yet there is nothing more frequent; notwithstanding the daily examples of punishment by death inflicted upon them; for I do not remember any Sessions for these half dozen years last past, wherein there hath not been at least one, if not more Tryed for this Bloody Crime. The present Prisoner was Servant to a Gentlewoman of good worth, and had behaved her self with that diligence and modesty, that she had gained much upon the Affections and good opinion of the Family, so that they had no mistrust of her; though when she had been privately Delivered, and disposed of her Child, she was taken notice of to be ill, and some Feminine symptomes appeared. But the same at last increasing, a Midwife was sent for; who examining and enquiring into Circumstances, concluded her to have been delivered of a Child, and charging her with it, she ingenuously confest it, and that it was in a void Garret, near the room she lay in, where they found it buried under certain Tiles and Rubbish. She then and now alleged that it was stillborn; but consenting that she was never Married and the Statute making it Death for a Woman to be delivered of a Bastard-Child, without witness or discovering it; and the Midwife, though she could not positively affrim that she had gone her full time, yet acknowledging the Infant had both Hair and Nails, she was Convicted, and received Sentence of death.[2]

The *OBSP* recorded nine cases of infanticide from January 16, 1685 to January 13, 1688. Six of the nine cases

ended with convictions, a rate comparable to earlier seventeenth-century rates in both England and New England. Of
the nine cases, six fell under the guidelines of 21 James I,
c. 27, and, of these six, four led to guilty verdicts. All the
nine accused were women, and all but one, a nurse who was
acquitted, were mothers of the victims. Spinster Jane Longworth tried to convince the jury that the smallpox had de-
ranged her, but concealment of her dead female bastard
infant in a trunk told against her. Elizabeth Stooke declared
that she was never pregnant, but examination by a jury of
midwives showed a recent delivery, and she was condemned. Katherine Brown admitted the delivery, but her
claim that the baby was born dead was "in no ways credited." Anne Philmore, an "ill-tempered woman" had other
children and a husband and was not judged under the statute, but a jury found her guilty of drowning her nine-week-
old baby, John. Servant Ann Trabern confessed to throwing
her newborn into a "bog house" (another word for a "privy
vault" or "house of office"); she was sentenced to be executed. Sinah Jones was believed to be insane when she suffocated her newborn bastard boy in a trunk, but the "statute
was read" and she was convicted of murder. It remained
within the power of the justices to seek her pardon from
the crown. To these women, and the crowds who doted
upon such events, the ordinary of the Old Bailey preached
a somber sermon. The Rev. Samuel Smith warned all: "take
heed of such libertinism, which pretends an easy way to
heaven, as if Christ had fulfilled all necessary duty in order
[to bring] salvation to your hand, and had left you at liberty,
to indulge the lusts of the flesh. . . . Suspect those things
most which are agreeable to your carnal desires."[3]

But even as the hangman saw these unfortunate women
off, a few defendants were finding defenses against the statute based on preparation for the child. On December 17,
1673, Ann Jewring pleaded her innocence of infanticide using evidence that she had made linen for her infant before
its birth. She was a single woman and had concealed her
pregnancy, the delivery of the child, and its death. The

corpse was discovered hidden in a box, but the coroner's jury did not charge her with the crime. In effect, she had pleaded a benefit-of-linen against the letter of the statute. There is no way of knowing how popular or effective this line of defense was before 1700, but after that date, benefit-of-linen, in the absence of evidence of violence upon the corpse, almost guaranteed an eventual acquittal in newborn bastard death trials. Word of this must have been widely disseminated. In 1718, a year for which the *OBSP* appear complete, there were six cases of infanticide. In five of these, the mothers of dead newborn bastards pleaded benefit-of-linen, and all were acquitted. The reporter noted when defendants had linen, and the linen was brought into court. In September 1722, widow Ann Morris defiantly told the court that she had no linen for her dead female bastard infant, knowing it was a telling point against her. In every case in the 1720s in which the defendant could produce linen prepared before labor, the jury acquitted the defendant. When Mercy Hamby tried to use this defense before a Middlesex judge and jury in 1734, however, it was discovered that she had borrowed the linen "from a neighbor" after the crime was committed. The statute was read to the jury, and she was convicted of murdering her newborn female bastard.[4]

Juries were also swayed by other pleas from unwed mothers accused of murdering their newborns. A want-of-help defense was common and often effective. Prior arrangement with a midwife, cries for help drowned out by passing carriages, a mistakenly locked door, a sudden illness preventing the solicitation of assistance, or a fall on the way to obtain help, buttressed suspects' cases. Want-of help might also occasion a verdict of not guilty of murder, but guilty of negligence. Failure to tie off umbilical cords, inability to stop the fall of a child onto a rough floor or into a bucket were not presumed to show murderous intent but a lack of skill or self-possession. Elizabeth Parker was acquitted when she convinced a jury that she tried to cut the umbilical cord of her newborn and missed. Pleasant Bateman's male bastard infant fell into a pan of water during a secret delivery, and its mother, claiming illness at that time, won a not-guilty verdict. Midwives, testifying that the child was premature or had closed fists, indicating stillbirth, were invaluable aides to the defendant in these cases. Murder required the victim to be *in rerum natura,* and evidence on the question of viability was therefore relevant to the murder charge. Servants with "good reputation" like Sarah Banestly were believed in their own defense when they pleaded want-of-help, though cold logic might designate them as likely candidates to preserve their reputations with covert infanticide.[5]

Pleas of accidental death or death due to the mother's medical incapacity were also credited. Defendants claimed that they had fallen shortly before or during labor, damaging the child before delivery. Temporary "fits," in which women went "out of their senses," became successful defenses when coupled with benefit-of-linen. Parker, for example, was found mentally incapacitated when she missed her son's umbilical cord and inflicted a large wound in his neck. In such cases, temporary insanity had become a legitimate defense, leading to a verdict of not guilty in the court. More often, women pleaded ignorance of the imminence of delivery. Their newborns fell from them when they sat upon the vault, and they did not know, or were too weak, to save the infants. Ann Jones claimed that she did not realize she was in labor when she went to the vault and lost her male bastard infant. The child was discovered alive and full term, but it died shortly thereafter. She was acquitted. If the child fell directly from the mother, instead of being murdered elsewhere and then concealed in the privy vault, there was no premeditation. Such accidents were possible. Labor pains can resemble those of a bowel movement, and a weakened, sick, or panicky new mother might lose a newborn into a vault, as Anne Haywood claimed in her successful defense at the Middlesex quarter sessions. Eighteenth-century jurors (unlike their seventeenth-century predecessors) were willing to believe that signs of violence, bruises or cuts, might result from the fall into the vault, rather than prior assault upon the child.[6]

Overall, juries were now as likely to favor the defendant, as early seventeenth-century juries were ready to condemn her. Eighteenth-century suspects concealed the corpses of bastard babies in trunks, pails, haystacks, stairwells, vaults, and coalbins in violation of the infanticide statute. Nevertheless, between 1714 and 1722, London and Middlesex juries disregarded the statute and found only four neonaticide defendants out of 22 to be guilty. This conviction rate was as far below 50 percent as the rate for the period between 1614 and 1622 was above 50 percent. Conviction for neonaticide became less probable than conviction for the murder of older children—a very different state of affairs from the preceding century. Of the five cases of older children murdered between 1714 and 1722, two ended in manslaughter verdicts (an idiot sister had drowned her two-year-old brother, and an older brother had fatally beaten his 2½-year-old sister), and three cases (involving passers-by and a nurse) ended in acquittals. In the 13 cases of concealment of dead newborn bastards coming to the Old Bailey between 1764 and 1784, 12 ended in acquittal, despite the fact that all 13 defendants violated the strictures of the statute. Ten cases of older infant murder were disposed of by the court; six with acquittals and four with convictions for manslaughter. In two of the guilty verdicts, cart drivers had fled the scene of their accidental killing of a child. An insane married women had killed her older child, and a boy had killed another with a rock. Those acquitted of murdering older children included a schoolmaster and a constable accused of fatal beatings of children. Two coachmen were acquitted of careless driving. Coroner's inquests presented these drivers for murder when the coroner's jury felt that the driver was at fault. About one of these per year appear in the *OBSP* and half of the defendants were found guilty of manslaughter, though none was convicted of murder. These deaths were part of an increasing number of violent traffic fatalities in the city. London draymen were not noted for their caution, and the small number of infant traffic deaths coming to the Middlesex goal delivery sessions suggests that only the worse offenders were prosecuted. The number of prosecutions for vehicular homicides of children, in modern terminology, did increase slightly over the course of the century as other infanticide indictments declined, until this form of child murder became the most numerous nonparental cause of the crime. Four married people, including a husband and wife, were found to have lost their infants through accidental causes. The 1624 statute no longer placed mothers of dead bastards defendants in greater jeopardy than would a simple murder charge. All of the bastard neonaticide cases in eighteenth-century London and Middlesex discussed above are summarized in Table 3.1.

In at least two of the acquittals after 1764, the defendant was represented by counsel. Spinster Ann Spinton had counsel to speak for her in a 1771 trial for neonaticide. The jury accepted her story of a miscarriage, followed by disposal of the remains down a privy vault. Technically, the case could have been decided the other way under the statute, for no one could swear that the infant was born dead. In 1784, counsel helped unmarried servant Elizabeth Curtis to convince a court that her bastard female infant had bled to death at birth while its mother lay helpless to save it. The right to counsel was limited to those who could afford it, which cannot have included many poor unwed infanticide defendants, and the precise role that counsel played in the Spinton and Curtis cases cannot be determined from the *OBSP*. Both women were acquitted, but so were all others in their position during these years without the assistance of counsel. In any event, the court expected the burden of the defense to rest upon the accused, not upon her counsel. She remained her own best witness. The basic lines of defense in infanticide cases had been introduced and had become successful at the beginning of the century, before lawyers intervened in these trials. The coming of legal assistance of their own choosing may have comforted the accused in in-

Table 3.1
Infanticide Conviction and Acquittal, from OBSP,
Middlesex and London, 1707–1727, 1764–1787, for those cases falling
under 21 James I, c. 27

Period	Not Guilty	Guilty
1707–1709	2	3
1710–	3	0
1713–	1	0
1716–	7	0
1719–	12	1
1722–	3	3
1725–1727	5	0
1764–1766	2	1
1767–	2	0
1770–	4	0
1773–	0	0
1776–	1	0
1779–	4	0
1782–	2	0
1785–1787	1	0
Totals	49	8

fanticide cases, but cannot have been the cause of the decline in convictions.[7]

In neighboring Surrey country, whose northern parts included the London docks at Southwark, a similar pattern of declining convictions for the crime of infanticide existed. One such case occured in March 1774. Mary Clifton, a servant, was accused of going off to have a female bastard child and returning to bury its corpse in her master's yard. The child was full term and had a small mark about its right eye. Mary had resumed her normal duties quickly after birth to avoid suspicion. Her master and mistress stood by her, but a doctor testified that she had recently delivered a baby. When confronted with this evidence, she admitted that she had the child, claimed she had cried out for help, and proved that she had sent for linen during confinement and labor. A midwife called to testify proved helpful to the defense. She proved her credentials for giving technical evidence that the child might have been stillborn by answering the judge's query: "Have you a great deal of practice" with "I hope so, I could not have maintained myself else." The doctor's performance of a test for live birth, submerging the lungs of the child in water, proved positive, but was discounted by the judge. Mary was acquitted, despite violation of the statute, a clear motive and opportunity for the crime, as well as having lied earlier about her condition. After 1750, hers was the typical result in Surrey courts.[8]

The same gradual but clearly discernible lessening of the percentage of convictions can be found in Essex at the end of the seventeenth-century and the opening decade of the eighteenth. Between 1685 and 1714, there were 22 cases of infanticide falling under the statute prosecuted at the Essex assizes, in which ten defendants were found guilty. Breaking these cases into two groups at the chronological midpoint of the period, between 1685 and 1700 and 1700 and 1714, shows that seven of 12 cases occurring in the earlier years ended in guilty verdicts, while only three of ten led to convictions in the later years. Six other cases of infant murder were resolved by the courts, in which two married couples were convicted for killing off their older children, and four married people were acquitted on the same charge.[9]

The same pattern of deliberate disregard for the Jacobean statute appears in Massachusetts courts after 1730. Of the 20 cases of infanticide fitting the statute in that colony between 1730 and 1780, only one led to conviction, that of Rebecca Chamblit. In almost all of these cases, the jury was informed of the Massachusetts law of 1696, but refused to convict upon it. A number of cases illustrate the jurors' aversion to the statute, and inversely, their willingness to convict for murder in infanticides not governed by the statute. Flora, a black slave woman, was accused of drowning her newborn in a privy vault. The father, another slave of the same master, lived with her by the consent of their owner. The jury asked for instruction in a special verdict. If Flora was a spinster, they would convict on the statute; if she was in some sense married, they would acquit her. The court ruled her not guilty, showing the justices' aversion to the cold formality of the statute, although the king's attorney had read it to the jury. When Patience, an Indian woman married to Boston, the black servant of Elisha Thatcher, was tried for the murder of her seven-week-old boy in 1732, she was acquitted. Three years later another trial jury in Falmouth found her guilty of beating and drowning the eight-year-old son of Benjamin Trott, and the court sentenced her to death. Between 1730 and 1780, three of the 11 suspects of murder of older infants were convicted. Charges of the murder of one's own bastard newborn were dismissed, except when the evidence presented fit the common law of murder. New England women tried only upon the infanticide statutes of 1696 and 1699 were safe, unless, as in any other murder, premeditation and cause of death could be established.[10]

The changing rates of convictions was so striking, in part, because the law itself had not been revised. In 1707, *Bond's Complete Guide for Justices of the Peace* repeated the kite case and named the statute of 1624 as the controlling law in matters of proof. Hale's *Pleas of the Crown* gave similar instructions. Blackstone, Gilbert, and other legal writers repeated these comments. The statute was read to juries when appropriate, but it failed to move them. Perhaps the severity of the penalty, the absence of an alternative to capital punishment for proof of mere concealment, made juries loathe to convict and judges hesitant to press for conviction when stillbirth or accident were possible. Not long before, however, the unavailability of lesser penalties had not stood in the way of a far higher percentage of convictions. Broader answers are needed to the puzzle of declining conviction rates. A natural first place to look is at the outcome of other homicide trials.[11]

A possible explanation for the fall in infanticide convictions was jurors' growing refusal to convict defendants in all murder cases. The trial verdicts for murder and manslaughter in eighteenth-century Middlesex England are summarized in Table 3.2.

Table 3.2
Murder Conviction Rates
of Those Charged,
Middlesex, 1685–1776 [a]

Period	Guilty of Murder	Not Guilty	Reduced to Guilty of Manslaughter
1685–1687	16	23	21
1714–1716	6	16	16
1724–1726	6	13	11
1764–1766	4	9	1
1774–1776	3	7	11

[a] Infanticide cases are excluded.

The rate of conviction for murder declined over this period, though not so steeply as that of infanticide, nor to so low a level. The difference was partly due to the tendency of juries to find a defendant charged with murder guilty of the noncapital offense of manslaughter, rather than to acquit the defendant entirely. Juries lacked that option in infanticide cases. In Elizabeth Curtis' case (1784), for example, the judge instructed the jury that "because there can be no provocation [infanticide] cannot be manslaughter." If one treats the manslaughter verdicts in murder cases as if they were verdicts of not guilty—in effect as a measure of the mercifulness which juries could not extend in infanticide trials because juries could not reduce the charge in the latter—one finds declines in percentages of conviction for murder of adults closer, though not quite equal, to those for infanticide.[12]

Essex assize files from the beginning of the eighteenth century show that the murder conviction rates in Middlesex were not unique to metropolitan London. If one regards "guilty of manslaughter" verdicts as guilty verdicts, there appears an irregular and barely visible lessening of the severity of conviction rates, from about a half, to slightly less than a half. If one supposes that the murder suspect would

Table 3.3
Murder Conviction Rates
of Those Charged,
Essex, 1685–1714[a]

Period	Guilty	Not Guilty	Reduced to Guilty of Manslaughter
1685–1689	0	4	4
1690–1694	3	7	3
1695–1699	2	3	0
1700–1704	2	1	3
1705–1709	1	1	1
1710–1714	1	5	1

[a] Infanticide cases are excluded.

have been acquitted had the lesser charge of manslaughter not been available, one sees a definite decline in conviction rates.

The drop in percentages of conviction for murder of adults in the Massachusetts superior court resembles that of the English assizes in its shape, although the precise figures are somewhat different. In Massachusetts, the conviction rates for murder charges dropped from about 50 percent before 1729 to about 30 percent from 1730 to 1780. This decline in the conviction rate does not quite equal that for neonaticides, which in Massachusetts between 1730 and 1780 was but 8.7 percent. The number of cases in the 1770s in which murder of an adult was penalized with a sentence for manslaughter, if added to the not guilty verdicts, would give a conviction rate of nine out of 48 cases, or 18.75 percent, closer still to the infanticide conviction rate for the whole period between 1730 and 1780.

When seventeenth-century infanticide juries had doubts about premeditation, they resolved them in favor of conviction. Seventeenth-century infanticide conviction rates were equal to combined eighteenth-century murder conviction and murder-reduced-to-manslaughter rates. When similar doubts disturbed eighteenth-century infanticide juries, they resolved them in favor of acquittal at a rate even greater than the combined percentages of murder of adults ending in acquittals and verdicts of murder reduced to manslaughter. These statistics lead to the conclusion that eighteenth-century juries were more lenient in infanticide cases than in murders involving adult victims. The decline in conviction percentages for infanticide came earlier in the century, was steeper, and fell to a lower level, than those for adult murder, even if one counts verdicts of guilty of manslaughter as acquittals in adult murder cases. While the rates of convictions of all of these crimes were falling, the differences between conviction rates for infanticide and those for other homicides mark the former as a special phenomenon.

Judges were moving in the same direction as juries. In infanticide cases at the Old Bailey, judges had begun to instruct juries to be certain that the neonatal victim was actually alive when the supposed violence was done to it. Judges there also refused to accept without question the floating of victims' lungs as proof of live birth. These rulings inevitably led to acquittals by the jury. Judicial mercy was not similarly extended to those convicted of murder of an adult. In Middlesex, England, the gibbets were crowded with murderers throughout the eighteenth century. Capital sentences for thefts and burglaries were frequently converted into transportation, but the murderer could expect little mercy. Table 3.4 illustrates this somber fact. If mercy was not given to murderers generally, but only to infanti-

Table 3.4
Murder Convictions and Executions,
London and Middlesex, *1707–1726, 1767–1796*

Period	Convicted	Executed
1707–1716	7	6
1717–1726	9	9
1767–1776	39	34
1777–1786	17	16
1787–1796	19	18

cide suspects, its source must lie elsewhere than in juries' or judges' compassion for homicide defendants.[13]

The mercy of eighteenth-century trial judges and juries in infanticide cases perhaps reflected a sense of the diminished threat of crimes like infanticide to the social order. The eighteenth-century Englishman was surrounded by crime and nowhere more visibly than in London and its environs. Throughout the 1700s the number of criminal indictments had steadily risen, keeping pace with overcrowding and deprivation of the poor within the city. The total of indictments for all crimes in the OBSP rose from 495 in 1726, to 539 in 1741, 588 in 1771, 910 in 1785, and 930 in 1786. This was an 88 percent rise overall, when the population in the greater London area rose but 11 percent. (Some of this increase in crime must be attributed to better reporting of offenses, but the perception of rising crime, well-mirrored by these figures, is what influenced juries.) City criminal magistrate Henry Fielding, no timid soul, reported "There is not a street in Westminster which doth not swarm all day with beggars, and all night with thieves."[14]

Nevertheless—an important exception—the number of indictments for homicide did not keep pace with other criminal prosecutions. Between 1685 and 1714, Old Bailey jurors heard from 12 to 17 cases of murder per year from a population of about 580,000—an indictment rate of 25.8 cases per hundred thousand people. By 1775, the *OBSP* reported about eight cases a year of murder, for a population slightly less than 650,000—an indictment rate of 10.8 per hundred thousand. Fewer indictments for murder meant that fewer jurors were likely to see and hear about murders even if, as was the case, they served more than once on the London or Middlesex trial or grand juries. Fewer cases made murder a less immediately threatening crime. Infanticide indictments declined slightly less steeply, but the drop was significant. Again, not all of this population was at risk to commit infanticide. If a corrective to the crime rate—as opposed to the rate of indictment we have been discussing—were to be calculated, it would account for the

32–34 percent of the population under nine years of age in England. The precise size of this multiplier would vary with the age composition of the population. If the unknown number of infanticides varied as a function of the population under the age of nine, the number of indictments might also vary as a function of population composition. In the period we are studying this variation would not be large, because infanticide was not a widespread form of covert birth control.

The indictments for infanticide decreased from .571 per hundred thousand people per year between 1670 and 1700, to .436 from 1701 to 1730, to .375 from 1731 to 1750, to .283 from 1751 to 1770, in London and Middlesex courts. Surrey court records reveal that from 1660 to 1720, about one infanticide case per year made its way to the assizes. From 1720 through 1802, a total of only 15 bills of indictment for infanticide reached Surrey grand juries. Over this time, the population of the county had more than doubled. While the average number of infanticide cases heard each decade by the superior court of judicature in Massachusetts remained about the same from 1700 to 1780, the population of the colony went from 70,000 to over 300,000. The Massachusetts indictment rate, by the 1770s, was about .18 per hundred thousand, down from .775 for the early 1700s, which, in turn, had a lower rate than the 1.41 of the 1680s and 1690s. With infanticide apparently in eclipse, experienced jurors might conclude that leniency in a particular case might not be dangerous to society as a whole or likely to encourage a flood of similar crimes in the future.[15]

The decline in the indictment rate probably reflected a combination of a diminished rate of actual commission of infanticide and an increase in sympathy for the rumored infanticidal parent. The first of these influences can only be measured approximately. The steep and steady fall in the rate of prosecutions means that fewer cases were brought to the courts. In a period of stable criminal procedures and law, such a decline strongly implies that fewer offenses were reported to authorities. There is some evidence that the decrease in reports of cases mirrored an actual reduction of infanticides. Between 1788 and 1829, the coroners for the city of London gave verdicts of infanticide upon examination of 53 corpses. For these 41 years at the turn of the century there were thus 1.3 reported cases of infanticide per year. This does not include geater London, but the number is quite comparable to the number of prosecutions—almost one per year—brought before the jurors "for the City." It appears that, during the period when prosecutions for infanticide were declining, they were nonetheless being commenced in nearly every instance in which a suspected case of infanticide came to the attention of a coroner.[16]

There exists literary and documentary evidence to corroborate the supposition that mothers were becoming more concerned with the emotional nurturing of their offspring, and would thus be less likely to commit infanticide. The extent to which such effective mothering percolated down from the upper and middle classes of late eighteenth-century English and American society to the poor is discussed in Chapter 5, but the broad outline of the growth of sentimental nurturing does fit the view that crimes of infanticide were decreasing. Shortly before the end of the eighteenth-century, William Wordsworth imagined the last thoughts of a sick and abandoned young North American Indian mother:

> My Child! they gave thee to another,
> A woman who was not thy mother.
> When from my arms my Babe they took,
> On me how strangely did he look!
> Through his whole body something ran,
> A strange working did I see:
> —As if he strove to be a man,
> That he might pull the sledge for me:
> And then he stretched his arms, how wild!
> Oh mercy! like a helpless child.

These were the Indians that Wordsworth's ancestors criticized for practicing infanticide, but this Indian mother's thoughts were as far from that act as romantic sentimentality could move them. She loved her child and, in that love, clung to a vestige of life. In "The Prelude," Wordsworth celebrated childhood and motherhood together, rejoicing in the union of the two:

> blest the Babe,
> Nursed in his Mother's arms, who sinks to sleep
> Rocked on his Mother's breast; who with his soul
> Drinks in the feelings of his Mother's eye!
> For him in one dear Presence, there exists
> A virtue which irradiates and exalts
> Objects through widest intercourse of sense;
> No outcast he, bewildered and depressed:
> Along his infant veins are interfused
> The gravitation and the filial bond
> Of nature that connect him with the world.

Poetry like this might well have signalled the appearance of a new era in parenthood.[17]

Changing attitudes toward parenthood followed changes in well-to-do eighteenth-century family life. Whether through an improvement in the standard of living, or from some deeper wellspring of human emotion, attitudes toward the rearing of children were changing. Perhaps the forces which had disrupted the social harmony of the early modern village, forces which had led to the campaign against witchcraft and infanticide, were forming a new pattern of social convention. Nuclear families were not novel, but the attention lavished upon the children in their midst was unlike that shown to earlier generations. Mortality rates of children had begun their decline. Wet nursing was going out of fashion. Infant medical care, by discontinuing swaddling, purges, confining harnesses, and other restrictive measures, was taking on its modern form. Evidence from diaries and letters also suggests that families were closer and more affective in the post-1700 era than they had been in earlier generations.[18]

The new social valuation of the child encouraged mothers to give more attention to infants. In this respect, the middle and upper classes provided a model. J. H. Plumb has concluded that "from what we do know, there can be no doubt that the children's world of the 18th century—at least for those born higher up the social scale than the laboring poor—changed dramatically." Expenditures for schools, the appearance of children's books written for the children themselves, and fashions and toys for the young market, all showed increasing adult concern for the pleasure of children. New England colonial parents were constantly being warned by magistrates and clergymen against the excesses of doting affection for their children, a certain evidence that such excesses were growing. Something of this emotional and material expenditure very probably seeped down to some less-fortunate parents of children.[19]

Even if new attitudes toward raising children had little impact on the way the poor treated their children, the new views of motherhood in particular, and the growth of romantic sentimentality in general, almost surely had a potent effect upon the attitudes of judges and jurors sitting in infanticide cases. In matters of sexual morality, that signal of infanticidal guilt for earlier generations of judges and juries, courts were becoming less severe. Although officials in England and New England continued to rail at incontinence, the weakened control that parents had over their older children undermined the officials' power to enforce sexual regularity. By the late eighteenth century in New England, "the experience of law enforcement in America as well as intellectual influences combined to suggest practical limits to what the law could accomplish in enforcement of morals."[20]

Evidence at the English assizes and quarter sessions, or the colonial superior courts, that an infant was a bastard, or that its mother had violated the code of sexual proprieties in some other way, no longer had the power to induce juries to presume guilt for the far weightier crime of murder. By the 1690s, the Essex County quarter sessions recorded an average of 13 prosecutions for bastardy each year—totals larger than at the beginning of the century—but infanticide conviction rates were declining. The population of the county had grown to about 168,000 from 70,000, explaining the increase in bastardy cases, and at the same time underlining the lack of relationship between bastardy prosecution and infanticide conviction in the courts. In mid-eighteenth-century London, the Mansion House justice court, where the lord mayor's magistrates dispensed justice and took money for recognizances, registered about ten bastardy warrants each month. The Guildhall magistrates court, situated in a less-impoverished part of the city of London, heard at least one parish complaint each month for support for a bastard born to a poor parishioner. The justices of the peace of the county of Middlesex, whose jurisdiction included those fathers unwilling to pay child support to the parish, issued orders for at least ten of these cases yearly during the later eighteenth century, but infanticide convictions steadily declined. In England, premarital pregnancy leaped from a fairly stable level of slightly under 20 percent of all first births between 1650 and 1725 to stable levels of over 40 percent by 1775. Jurors could hardly fail to know that premarital and sexual activities were increasing greatly, but refused to use infanticide verdicts to penalize female sexual transgressors accused of the former offense. Increasingly common, sexual transgressions were less stigmatizing. For all the bastardy cases, complaints, orders, and warrants, the conviction of women known to have concealed their dead bastard newborns steadily declined in New England, Essex and Middlesex counties, England, and the city of London.[21]

Under the influence of these new attitudes, it was the quality of maternal love that became the issue for jurors at infanticide trials, not details of legitimacy or previous sexual experience. A mother who said she loved her bastard child could be believed, and such avowals disproved evil intent. In February 1769, Elizabeth Grindall, a widow, stood indicted at the Old Bailey for casting her 18-month-old daughter into the New River. While witnesses and physical evidence indicated that she might have intended to dispose of the child, testimony about her earlier tender ministrations toward it helped win her acquittal. Her brother-in-law swore in her defense, "She loved the child even to distraction: no woman in the world could love a child better." Elizabeth Harris was a servant, nurse, and wife accused of strangling her newborn child and hiding the body in a box. In May, 1781, a Middlesex, English jury acquitted her of the murder charge, despite proof of violence to the infant, when the jurors heard how she cried at the discovery of her little one. They accepted her defense: Out of her senses at the time of birth, she had wounded the child in the neck while trying to untangle the umbilical cord.[22]

As attitudes of judges and jurors toward infanticide suspects softened, legal reformers began to argue for repeal of the infanticide statute of 1624. In 1772, Edmund Burke, Charles James Fox, and others moved in the house of commons that 21 James I c. 27 be repealed. In opposition, it was argued that proof of the crime was very difficult because of concealment of the birth and the corpse. The crime was so easily committed it was akin to the use of an undetectable poison. The opponents of the resolution maintained that the government would be right in prohibiting the mere possession of such a poison. Other nations, they continued, had such laws, including France and Denmark. Rejoinders by Burke and Fox showed awareness of both the experience of the courts and the rising appreciation of maternal sentiment:

> They said, that in the case of women having bastard children, the common [and] statute laws were inconsistent; that the common law subjected to a fine, to a month's imprisonment, and the flagellation; that this institution necessarily rendered the having of a bastard child infamous; that the dread of infamy necessarily caused concealment; that the statute law, in opposition to all this, made concealment capital; that every mother, who had not at least one witness to prove, that her child, if it was dead, was born dead, or died naturally, must

be hanged; that nothing could be more unjust, or inconsistent with the principles of all law, than first to force a woman through modesty to concealment, and then to hang her for that concealment; that it was infinitely better that ten guilty persons should escape, than an innocent person should suffer; that this law, on the contrary, asserted it to be better, that ten innocent persons should be hanged, than one guilty person should escape; that as to the comparison of the subtle poison, it was not applicable to the present case; that a law, rendering the possession of such a poison capital, was not defensible, except it could be proved impossible that the possessor should have it for any good purpose; that this condition was wanting in the present case; that the concealment of the birth of a bastard might proceed from the best causes, from real modesty and virtue; that nothing could more strongly prove the absurdity and inexpediency of the law, than the impossibility of putting it in execution, under which the judges found themselves; that laws were made to be executed, not dispensed with; that the example of Denmark and France, despotic countries, ought to be no model for us; that this observation only proved, that the law of France ought not to be that of England; that the parliament which made this law was not infallible; that, while all due praise was allowed to legitimate children, it was not just to give a squeeze in the neck to bastards; and that humanity and justice pleaded strongly for the alteration contended for.[23]

Burke and Fox's infanticide bill echoed the arguments of opponents of indiscriminant capital punishment. The consensus of reformers like Romilly and Colquhoun and magistrates like Fielding was that capital punishment should be reserved only for a few crimes, not including concealment of bastardy. Blackstone, no radical reformer, believed in capital punishment for murders, but went on, "Yet, though in this instance we may glory in the wisdom of the English law, we shall find it more difficult to justify the frequency of capital punishment to be found therein." The infanticide statute of 1624 had the practical effect of making concealment of the death of one's bastard infant a capital offense—a penalty which Blackstone had found particularly severe.

Legal essayist Michael Foster agreed. In 1762, he noted that "From the delicacy of their Frame [women] seem to be the most susceptible of Human Passions. . . ." If concealment of a stillborn bastard by a distraught, frail, emotionally unstable young mother was a capital offense, then the law discriminated against the weaker sex. As Blackstone and Foster must have known, assize and quarter sessions juries were finding ways to credit the accounts of those young women who claimed to have lost their bastard children through natural or accidental means.[24]

The Burke and Fox resolution failed, but juries continued to flout the letter of the law. Finally, in 1803, Chief Justice Lord Ellenborough proposed the repeal of the infanticide statute as one item in an omnibus crime bill (43 Geo. III, c. 58). The bill was read for the first time in the lords on March 28, 1803, and in the commons on May 18. After amendments in the commons were agreed to in the lords, the bill had its final reading on June 18, and was assented to by the king on June 24. The act made a number of crimes capital, including abortion with drugs, malicious shooting, and certain arsons. It was a harsh bill, befitting Ellenborough's dim view of crime and criminals. His justification for the repeal of the infanticide law fits his reputation as a man of little sympathy for the accused:

> to relieve the judges from the difficulties they labor under in respect to the trial of women indicted for childmurder, in the case of bastards. At present the judges were obliged to train the law for the sake of lenity, and to admit the lightest suggestion that the child was stillborn as evidence of the fact.

Instead, Ellenborough provided that should prosecution for murder fail upon proof that the child was not born alive, the woman might still receive up to two years in prison if the jury found her guilty of concealing the birth. A direct prosecution for concealment only, without a prior trial for murder, became possible in 1829 (9 Geo. IV, c. 34).[25]

Whatever Ellenborough's purpose may have been, the bill made legal the leniency juries had been showing. At the

York county summer assizes of 1803, an immediate test of the new law appeared. A dead female infant was discovered in a hole on the moors, sewn in a cloth, without visible marks of violence and with an untied umbilical cord. The female infant was shown to a local surgeon. He testified that the child had been born alive and had been suffocated, as indicated by the swollen condition of the nose and mouth. Spinster Rebecca Beaumont was apprehended and found to have breasts full of milk, but she denied having had a child for the past two years. Although witnesses placed her in the vicinity of the child's makeshift grave at about the time of its concealment, she maintained her innocence to the end. Recalcitrance and a poor local reputation might once have earned her the death penalty, but under the new law, she was convicted only for concealment. The judge's final words, reported by a chapbook author, show the effect of the new laws:

> The judge, in summing up, observed, that by the indictment, the death was alleged to have arisen from wounds and bruises on the body of the child, and from suffocation; but there was no evidence before the jury to convince them that the death of the child arose from either of those causes. Mr. Scholes had described a bruise on the child's mouth, but here seemed no ground to conclude that that had caused its death. Should the jury be of opinion that the child had died by the cutting of its navel string, and the consequent effusion of blood, which from the evidence seemed to be most probable, the jury must be under the necessity of acquitting the prisoner under that indictment, whether they considered the cutting of the navel string to have been the effect of negligence or of design. The bleeding to death should have been charged in the indictment. But should the jury be of opinion, that the prisoner had been delivered of a child, and concealed its birth, of which there seemed little reason to doubt from the evidence, they should return a special verdict of that fact, and the prisoner would be punished for such concealment, under a late Act of Parliament.
>
> Verdict.—Not guilty of murder; but of having been delivered of a child, which, if born alive, would have been a bastard, and concealed its birth.

Beaumont was sentenced to two years in the house of correction at Wakefield, the maximum penalty under the law.[26]

Commentators on the new law were quick to explain its return to older conceptions of proof of murder. The jury was to determine whether the act of concealment actually led to the death, or whether, as in want-of-help cases, it was the mother's weakness, ignorance, or negligence that resulted in the death of the child. Murder required premeditation, making crucial the testimony of medical witnesses in these cases. If the mother called for help, or made preparations for the child, then there was no concealment, even if the delivery was not witnessed by another. The penalty for the separate crime of concealment of bastardy, it should be noted, applied even when stillbirth was proven. The loss of a premature child down a privy vault, for example, could lead to punishment for concealment of a bastard. If the infant was not found in a place of concealment, however, the mother could not be forced to answer for its whereabouts.[27]

In the two years following the modification of infanticide law, Middlesex and London courts heard three cases of bastard neonaticide. Christine Kirby was found not guilty of strangling her newborn female infant, "there being no evidence to prove that the child was born alive." Though the child was a bastard and the pregnancy was secret, no effort was made to prosecute her for concealment of birth. Ann Smith was acquitted of murder, but imprisoned for one year for dropping her newborn bastard into a privy vault. Though she had prepared linen—a telling point against the murder charge—she was reported "a very bad girl" by neighbors. Sarah Dixon received a two-year sentence for the concealment of her infant's death. She had denied her pregnancy and delivery to her mistress, and days after the birth tried to secret the corpse of the child in a pile of debris blocks from her house. The jury found that the infant died of natural causes, but Dixon's planned and persistent concealment was punished. In these and other trials after 1803, judges instructed jurors that neighbors' knowledge of illicit pregnancy was evidence of preparation for the child—a very different view from that taken by justices 200 years before. When penalties against concealment were invoked, they were directed not against the sexual offense of bastardy, but against the willful circumvention of law after the infant had died.[28]

Massachusetts' lawmakers had anticipated this sequence of statutes. In 1784 the commonwealth created the offense of concealment of the death of a bastard child:

> A woman who conceals the death of issue of her body, which if born alive would be illegitimate, so that it cannot be ascertained whether it was born dead or, if born alive, whether it was murdered, shall be punished by a fine of not more than one hundred dollars or by imprisonment for not more than one year.

This did not prevent either the indictment of a woman for both concealment and murder or conviction for the former offense after acquittal for the latter, although prosecutions for concealment were rare. When such cases did come to court, judges and juries were lenient. In June, 1799, a York county, Maine, grand jury handed up a true bill against Hannah Durgin for concealing the death of her female bastard. The evidence showed she had induced Ephraim Chick and his wife Phoebe to dispose of the corpse, the married couple "well knowing" that the child was a bastard and secretly born. Durgin first pleaded not guilty but then reversed herself. The judges at the supreme judicial court session sentenced her very lightly, to pay court costs and spend two weeks in gaol. James Sullivan, the attorney general and prosecutor for the commonwealth, then spoke with the judges and endorsed the indictment in his own hand: "On conference with the judges, having doubts whether on the statute an indictment can be maintained against the said Ephraim and Phoebe, he will prosecute no further on this indictment." It was one matter to prosecute accessories to murder, but quite another to take up the time of the high tribunal with accessories to the minor offense of concealing the death of a bastard. In 1808, the general assembly of Connecticut also divided the English infanticide law into its two components by enacting a statute similar to that of Massachusetts. Thus, in England and New England, the law, after nearly a century of divergence from popular sensibilities, again conformed to social attitudes toward the crime of infanticide.[29]

Part II

The Defendants

4

Suspects and Victims,
England and New England, 1558-1803

From the perspective of lawmakers, magistrates, and learned observers, one can loosely trace the parabolic course of infanticide cases in the courts, but the accused and their victims pass through the records as through a glass darkly. Who were these men and women, suspected of murdering their own offspring, or causing the deaths of children not related to them? What effect did the circumstances of the defendants' lives have upon the enforcement of the law? By combining quantitative methods and contemporary accounts, it is possible to establish the chief characteristics of those men and women brought to the dock for the crime. One can follow the typical offender, an unmarried young woman, accused of murdering her newborn, through the travail of indictment and trial.[1]

Cases in the criminal record do more than illuminate the crime; correlation of information on defendants and victims leads to sound generalizations. In tabulations of the number of cases in the preceding chapters, the single unit of analysis, the "case," was defined by the assize indictment. This was appropriate in assessing the effect that infanticide trials had upon judges, juries, commentators, and lawmakers. In the following cross tabulations of defendants' and victims' characteristics, the unit of analysis shifts from the "case" to the "defendant," two or three of whom might be indicted in a single case. The number of defendants is larger than the number of cases because very few defendants were charged with the crime more than once. To assure the historical validity of generalization, the analysis of groups of cases must be governed by the previous chapters' findings. One must not ignore differences between Tudor-Stuart cases and eighteenth-century English cases, or between Old World and New World defendants, if such differences do in fact exist. Instead, one must attempt an intensive investigation of each period defined in Part I.

In the years between 1558 and 1624, 139 defendants faced trial for infanticide in Essex, Hertford, Middlesex, and Sussex. The distribution of these defendants is Essex, 46; Herfordshire, 17; Middlesex, 35; and Sussex, 41. The Hertford record begins, not in 1558, but in 1573. The data for Middlesex, including the city of London and the outlying parishes, is spotty. Reliable records for that jurisdiction from 1606 to 1618, 11 years out of the 66 in our period, show 29 indictments, or roughly 2.7 cases a year. If this figure held for the entire period between 1558 to 1624, allowing for the steady rise in London population, one could surely expect more than 100 cases. Nevertheless, the missing data does not affect a comparison of the characteristics of cases and defendants unless a systematic bias caused the survival of records of the 12 defendants recorded in the years between 1558 and 1606 and 1619 and 1624, or the cases within the years 1607 and 1618 are unrepresentative of the larger period. The 47 cases in the Essex assize files between 1625 and 1650 were compared with the cases from Elizabethan and Jacobean courts. Defendants' sex, relationship to the victim, marital status, and occupation were coded, as were victims' legitimacy, age, and sex. In each case information on concealment, the cause of death, and the site of the crime was noted. The verdict of the trial jury completed the data card for each case.[2] Significant patterns

Table 4.1
Characteristics of Defendants and Victims
in Infanticide, 1558–1623[a]

Category	Absolute	Relative Frequency	Adjusted Frequency
Legitimacy	Frequency	(percent)	(percent)[b]
Legitimate	17	12.2	14.4
Illegitimate	101	72.7	85.6
Unknown	21	15.1	—
Total	139	100	100.0
Age of Victim			
Neonate	104	74.8	85.2
Under two	14	10.1	11.5
Under nine	4	2.9	3.3
Unknown	17	12.2	—
Total	139	100.0	100.0
Relationship of Defendant to Victim			
Parent	112	80.6	85.5
Caretaker	2	1.4	1.5
Other	17	12.2	13.0
Unknown	8	5.8	—
Total	139	100.0	100.0
Defendant's Sex			
Male	15	10.8	10.8
Female	124	89.2	89.2
Total	139	100.0	100.0
Defendant's Marital Status			
Married	25	18.0	21.0
Single	90	6.7	75.6
Widowed	4	2.9	3.4
Unknown	20	14.4	—
Total	139	100.0	100.0

[a] We have included in this table the "accessories" to the crime.
[b] The adjusted frequency is the percentage of each category when the "unknown" category is dropped out.

in the data for the period between 1558 and 1623 are summarized in Table 4.1.

Analysis of 47 cases from Essex from the years between 1625 and 1650 indicates that the Jacobean infanticide act had little impact on these patterns. The relative frequency of the illegitimacy of Essex victims after 1625 was 70.2 percent (adjusted frequency 76.7 percent, 43 cases coded); the victims were newborn 72.3 percent of the time (adjusted to 79.1 percent, 43 cases coded); the suspect was the parent in 87.2 percent of the cases, (adjusted to 89.1 percent, 46 cases were coded) and in 89.4 percent of the cases the defendant was female (all cases were coded). The defendants were single or widowed in 63.9 percent of the cases (adjusted to 75 percent when the "unknowns" are removed).

Infanticide was a crime for which women were indicted far more frequently than men. Of the defendants for the crime, almost 90 percent were women. This is almost exactly the opposite of the distribution of the sexes in murders and manslaughters of adult victims. In Essex, between 1603 and 1650, there were 117 cases of the murder or manslaughter of victims over the age of eight years, and 152 (91 percent) of the defendants in those 117 cases were male, while only 15 (9 percent) of the accused were female. From 1559 to 1602, the Sussex assizes heard 94 cases of the murder and manslaughter of adults, in which 90 (87 percent) of the defendants were men, and 13 (13 percent) were women. From 1612 to 1618, the Middlesex quarter sessions of the peace and general goal delivery courts disposed of murder and manslaughter cases involving 63 (88 percent) men and nine (12 percent) women. The almost mirrorlike contrast between female fatal assaults upon children and women's participation in the murder and manslaughter of adults can be attributed to female roles in society. Women did not engage as often as men in combats in the streets, on the roads, or in the marketplaces, but women performed almost all of the child care. When they felt anger, the nearest object was not another adult but a child, and, as the table reports, frequently their own child. It was in this sense inevitable that infanticide would be a woman's crime.

The vast preponderance of parents among the defendants, 81 percent of the unadjusted cases, indicates that infanticide was a domestic crime. Whether the victim was newborn or just under the age of discretion, the greatest danger of mortal violence to it lay within the family circle. To be sure, frightening stories of strangers murdering innocent babes flourished in this era. In 1646, John Doleman reported the suspicious disappearance of a child to Middlesex justice of the peace William Ashton. The child was seen in the neighborhood by a maid, and went off in the company of a local butcher's wife. A few days later, Doleman was taken ill by one of his landlady's meat pies, purchased from the butcher. He brought his fears to the justice of the peace. Chapbooks and ballads spread similar tales. Dell's case (1606), the slaying of a three-year-old boy by an elderly tavern-keeper and her adult son, was told in great detail by an anonymous pamphleteer. The keeper had promised to take care of the child, but murdered him instead. The *Children in the Wood* (1601), a popular ballad, described a wicked uncle's double child murder. The uncle was to rear the children, but led them into the woods and arranged their deaths. Later, the uncle died a cruel death. The balladeer concluded: "Of children that be fatherless,/ . . . yield to each his right,/Lest God with such like miserye/Your wicked minds requite." In later years, the *Complete Newgate Calendar* featured lurid tales of child murderers, like Tom Austin, who in 1694 butchered his aunt and her five young charges for the 60 pounds sterling in her dresser. The statistics suggest that these notorious crimes were atypical, in which case their dissemination may have served to warn rather than report. The stock characters in these cases—the haglike miscreant Anis Dell, the wild Austin and the unscrupulous butcher and uncle—were caricatures of villains.[3]

The concentration of defendants in the category of unmarried parent and the predominance of newborn children among the victims does not correspond to the proportion of these groups in the population of England. The inclusion of the murder of older infants in the data serves to underline the extent to which neonates were victims of parental

Table 4.2
Marital Status of Female Defendants
by Age of Victim, England, 1558–1623[a]

Age of Victim	Marital Status of Defendant			
	Married	Single	Widowed	
Neonate				
Actual count	11	101	5	117
Row percentage	9.4	86.3	4.3	90.0%
Column percentage	61.1	94.4	100.0	
Total percentage	8.5	77.7	3.8	
Under two				
Actual count	5	5	0	10
Row percentage	50.0	50.0	0.0	7.7%
Column percentage	27.8	4.7	0.0	
Total percentage	3.8	3.8	0.0	
Between two and eight				
Actual count	2	1	0	3
Row percentage	66.7	33.3	0.0	2.3%
Column percentage	11.1	0.9	0.0	
Total percentage	1.5	0.8	0.0	
	18	107	5	130
	13.8%	82.3%	3.5%	100.0%

[a] Cramer's $V = -.278$; significant at the 95 percent level.

violence. Though the matter of bastardy will receive more detail shortly, it is appropriate here to note that in these years on average no more than 4 to 5 percent of the yearly births were of bastards. Were premarital pregnancies added to these totals, the percentage of out-of-wedlock conceptions would still fall below 25 percent of the live births. Table 4.1 indicates that it was the unwed mothers of bastards who were the typical defendant, and newborn bastards the most likely victim. This relationship, then, requires special attention.[4]

Among the ranks of mothers suspected of infanticide, one expects and finds a negative statistical relationship between the married defendant and the neonatal victim. Married women were not accused of murdering their newborn babies; unmarried women were suspected of just that. The strength of association among these categories is moderately strong, and would be stronger but for the "skewedness" of the marginal totals. The disproportionate numbers of unmarried defendants and neonates has the statistical byproduct of artificially depressing the measures of association. When appropriate steps are taken to control for this skewing of the marginals, a much higher level of association emerges.

To remove the effect of marginals that are very uneven, we standardize the table. By dividing row totals and column totals through by a factor of 100/(marginal total) in successive cycles, in effect using the row and column percentages as our cell entries, we can refashion a table with an even distribution of marginal totals. To simplify standardization of Table 4.2, we collapse the three age categories into "neonate" and "older" than neonate, and the three marital status categories into "married" and "unmarried."

Table 4.2a
Marital Status By Age of Victim
After Collapsing Categories[a]

Age of Victim	Marital Status		
	Married	Unmarried	
Neonate	11	106	117
Older	7	6	13
Total	18	112	130

[a]For this table, phi = −.386.

After eight cycles of standardization, we obtain Table 4.2b. Its entries are the cell percentages of the standardized marginal totals. The "phi" coefficient is now −.556.

Table 4.2b
Marital Status By Age of Victim After Standardization[a]

	Marital Status		
Age of Victim	Married	Unmarried	
Neonate	21.8	78.2	100
Older	77.4	22.6	100
Total	99.2	100.8	

[a]Phi = −.556.

This is a strong negative association between marriage and neonaticide.[5]

Concealment was also strongly in evidence among the unmarried women accused of killing their newborns. Table 4.3 documents this relationship.

Table 4.3
Victim Age by Concealment, When the Victim
was Illegitimate, England, 1558–1623[a]

Was Victim Concealed?	Age of Victim			
	Neonate	Under Two	Under Nine	
Yes				
Actual count	32	2	0	34
Row percentage	94.1	5.9	0.0	75.6%
Column percentage	84.2	33.3	0.0	
Total percentage	71.1	4.4	0.0	
No				
Actual count	6	4	1	11
Row percentage	54.5	36.4	9.1	24.4%
Column percentage	15.8	66.7	100.0	
Total percentage	13.3	8.9	2.2	
	38	6	1	45
	84.4%	13.3%	2.2%	100.0%

[a]Cramer's V = .481; significant at the 99.5 percent level.

Although standardization would undoubtedly increase this association, its strength is already clear. One cannot know the extent to which suspicion of the motives of the unwed mother who concealed a dead infant was a self-fulfilling prophecy—that is, to what degree the criminal justice sys-

tem tended to focus upon the death of bastards and so
bring their mothers to court in larger numbers than a more
disinterested regard for the evidence would warrant.

Unmarried mothers did not always act alone in neonaticide. In 1565, a Sussex assize jury found Sybil Ellyot and
her husband William not guilty of murdering a newborn
male infant in a church orchard. Christine Grantham was
believed to be the culprit. A year later Grantham was convicted on this charge, but the Ellyots were found guilty as
accessories. Evidently, it was Grantham's baby that had been
strangled. The Ellyots may have been friends, or acting for
the father. Sissilye Linscale inadvertantly, as she testified before the York assize court, witnessed the birth of a bastard
child to her cousin Ann. With the help of Elizabeth Aggar,
another servant, Ann buried the child alive. Sissilye was
sworn to secrecy, but told her master anyway. Her evidence
failed to convince the trial jury, and all the women were
freed. The most frequent aider and abettor in the few
neonaticides involving accessories was the unwed mother's
own mother. In 1588, a coroner's jury in Sussex found
spinster Ursula Farmer and her mother, Alice Farmer, of
Rotherfield, not guilty of drowning a female child in a
spring. A year later, the assizes for the county heard the
cases of Mary Mouser and her mother Agnes, both indicted
for the murder of Mary's newborn daughter. The child's
throat was cut, and the trial jury found Mary guilty, but her
mother was freed. Fathers were included in indictments as
accessories and conspirators in the concealment of births,
but women bore the brunt of the prosecution. Fathers and
lovers were rarely convicted, even on those occasions when
a grand jury brought a true bill against them. When
Thomas Norton of Middlesex put his pregnant maid servant into a cold barn to bear her bastard and the child died,
for example, a coroner's jury charged him with murder, but
the judges delivered him by proclamation.[6]

Two features of the cases above deserve attention. First,
when more than one individual was involved, assistance was
likely to come from within the family. Mother and father, if

they were present and willing, might shelter a daughter from the magistrates. Far more important is the number of times infanticide was committed by a single woman, acting alone. This is very different from the pattern of women's participation in other crimes of violence. In all 35 of the assaults in which women took part in later Elizabethan Hertfordshire, for example, they had at least one accessory. In Stuart Middlesex, between 1613 and 1618, females accused of murder and manslaughter had accomplices in six of 11 cases. It cannot be denied that women who tried to murder their infants alone might have found concealment of the pregnancy, birth, and the crime itself far more difficult than women who had family or friends in the vicinity. The more support an infanticidal parent could draw from family, friends, and community, the safer she was after the crime. Nevertheless, the different rate at which married and unmarried women were convicted of the crime, after they had been indicted, shows that the jury continued to stress the connection between the social isolation of the unwed defendant and her willingness to commit infanticide. The juries' logic was sound. Infanticide, especially of newborns by women, was indeed a solitary crime, a crime which would have particular attraction to a woman without ties facing the legal penalties and social burdens of rearing a bastard.[7]

In court, the defendant's character and circumstantial proof of concealed pregnancy were almost as important as evidence of actual premeditation introduced against her. (The association between the verdict and these facts can be very complex, but it is possible to examine the effects of each fact upon the jurors' verdict while holding the effects of the other facts "constant." This we attempt in Appendix 1.) In part, the trial process drove judges and juries toward this course. Trial was speedy, a few hours at maximum in most cases, and the assize justices, theoretically charged with protecting the legal rights of all who stood accused, in practice often accelerated the pace of the proceedings. The defendant herself could not testify under oath, and there was no bar to testimony about her previous convictions or conduct. The jury could draw its own conclusions, finding ways to soften the law of homicide if it chose. In this context of harsh law, hurried judges, and independent-minded juries, circumstantial evidence became extremely important.[8]

Defendants found their reputation and the age and legitimacy of the supposed victim their best defense or their worst accuser. Justice Lambarde of Kent told court officers to discover if suspects were persons of "quality," if they had evil parents who had committed similar crimes, if they themselves were of an evil nature, or kept bad company, or had no job, or had ever been accused of a similar offense. When Dorothy Thorowgood was tried twice in three years for the suspicious deaths of successive newborn bastards, for example, the verdict of guilty in the second trial was all but inevitable. Wrightson has traced one Essex case in which a woman's evil reputation pursued her for two years, in and out of the courts.

A peculiarly striking case, which illustrates the complex filter of circumstances and relationships which lay between the committing of an offence and the making of a criminal indictment is that of Elizabeth Codwell, widow, of Terling, Essex. She bore a base child on 23 January 1643. The burial register of Terling for the same month contains the entry 'a base child of Elizabeth Codwell widow, whom she fathered upon Thomas Hanbury was born 23; stifled or killed by her the same day and conveyed away or buried by her procurement the 25th, the general fast day'. The widow, who enjoyed the aliases of Parsons and Hills, was a marginal member of the village community. She had come to Terling from Chelmsford as a servant in the late 1620s and her aliases may indicate that she was herself illegitimate. She was certainly mentally unstable. A paper endorsed 'Eliz: Cadwill lunatique' among the sessions bundles for 1628, contains an account of her examination by her master concerning 'what the cause was that she was so troubled and aflicted in mind'. She had apparently suffered from the attempts of an earlier master to seduce her and she regarded him as the author of the hallucinations of deaths' heads which disturbed her. The father of

her illegitimate child, Thomas Hanbury, was known in Terling as a drunkard and disorderly person. Behind the events
of 1643 may have lain a history of suffering and exploitation
and it seems very probably that she killed her child in one of
her fits of depression. On the morning of the child's birth
and death a justice of the peace, Sir Benjamin Ayloffe, was
sent for. Witnesses, one of whom had been present at her
examination in 1628, were subsequently examined on 2 February. Sir Benjamin, however, did not bind over the witnesses
to prosecute an indictment. This may have been partly out of
commiseration for Elizabeth's mental state and partly a result
of the fact that the emergencies of the Civil War meant that
sessions and assizes were suspended in Essex in 1643 and
1644. The matter lapsed and so it might have remained but
for the strength of one section of local opinion. In an otherwise undated letter of 16 July, probably 1645, the matter was
revived by John Stalham, minister of Terling and his ally
John Maidstone, a freeholder. They wrote to another justice,
Arthur Barnardiston that 'in as much as an unnaturall and
barbarous murther hath been committed in our parish . . .
the guilt whereof we are careful not to contract . . . we
thinke meet to advertsye you that the persons here after
named being summoned wil be able to evidence the busynes'.
There followed a list of witnesses and a request that they be
summoned quickly 'to the intent that so horrid a crime may
not escape the hand of justice'. Elizabeth Codwell was indicted on 17 July 1645 and sentenced to death, though she
was temporarily reprieved in view of the fact that she was
again pregnant. Whether she was eventually hanged is unknown.[9]

The mixture of reputation and circumstantial evidence
was made more potent when marks of violence could be
found on the victim. Of 16 married parents in Essex accused of murdering their infants between 1558 and 1623,
nine were convicted. Evidence of severe brutality to the
body of the victim was cited in eight of the nine indictments
that led to guilty verdicts. Typical among these, Dorcas
Tyndall cut her week-old child's throat. She was found
guilty, but insane, and died while in prison. Without signs
of violence on the victim, married suspects were not con-

victed, with one exception. Alice Carter was found guilty of poisoning her one-year-old baby. The clerk of the court marginally noted that the evidence seemed to him insufficient for the verdict, but poisoning was an especially repulsive crime to Englishmen. Evidence of bruises or cuts also damaged the defense when the child was a newborn bastard. When visible signs of violence to the infant were made evident to the jury, the likelihood of conviction rose from one in two times to four in five times. Cuts and bruises on bastard neonates might have resulted from accidents during or shortly after a delivery handled without assistance by a weak, frightened, and inexperienced young mother. Eighteenth-century English jurors credited such explanations; seventeenth-century trial juries did not.[10]

The distribution of personal characteristics and the typology of infanticides in New England closely paralleled the mother country. In New England, defendants fell into one of two distinct categories: the young woman suspected of concealing the birth and then murdering her illegitimate newborn and the married woman believed to have destroyed her older infant. For cases from the existing Massachusetts court records for the period between 1630 and 1780, the overall frequencies in Table 4.4 reflect this bimodal pattern.

By far, the most frequent victim was the illegitimate newborn; the most numerous suspects were parents. In New England as in the mother country, infanticide was a crime of women. There were 68 female defendants in murder cases in Massachusetts between 1680 and 1779; 66 of these women stood accused of infanticide (98%). There were 156 men tried for murder in the commonwealth during the same period; ten of these (7 percent) were suspects in infanticide cases. The facts of concealment, illegitimacy, and neonatal death were united in New England cases with even greater frequency than they came together in the English cases. In Chapter 2, we have already traced the impact of these combinations of evidence upon the verdicts of Puritan jurors. A statistical analysis of the effects of concealment,

Table 4.4
Infanticide Characteristics, Massachusetts, 1630–1780
(76 Defendants, 73 Victims, including two Pairs of Twins)

Category		Absolute Frequency	Relative Frequency (percent)	Adjusted Frequency (omitting unknowns) (percent)
Legitimacy [a]	Yes	16	21.9	23.9
	No	51	69.9	76.1
	Unknown	6	8.2	—
Victim Age	Neonate	52	71.2	72.2
	Under Two	10	13.7	13.9
	Under Nine	10	13.7	13.9
	Unknown	1	1.4	—
Defendants' [b]	Parent	64	84.2	85.3
Relation to	Caretaker	6	7.9	8.0
Victim	Other	5	6.6	6.7
	Unknown	1	1.3	—
Defendants' [b]	Male	10	13.2	13.2
Sex	Female	66	86.8	86.8
Defendants' [b]	Servant	15	19.7	31.9
Occupation	Other	32	42.1	68.1
	Unknown	29	38.2	—
Defendants' [b]	Married	23	30.3	34.8
Marital	Single	41	53.9	62.1
Status	Widowed	2	2.6	3.1
	Unknown	10	13.2	—

[a] In two cases the victim was the adulterous, hence illegitimate, offspring of a married woman: Smith's case (1698) and Fennison's case (1742). Both ended in guilty verdicts.

[b] Includes 71 principals and five accessories.

Table 4.5
Infanticide in Massachusetts and Middlesex, 1680–1780

	affirmative answer in percent			
Category	Massachusetts (65 Cases) (1680–1780)		Middlesex (87 Cases) (1685–1688, 1707–1727, 1733–1738, 1764–1780)	
Illegitimacy[c]?	78[a]	(95)[b]	68[a]	(97)[b]
Neonaticide?	74	(98)[b]	78	(100)[b]
Accused was parent of victim?	85	(99)[b]	81	(99)[b]
Accused was female?	86	(100)[b]	90	(100)[b]
Accused was servant?	33	(55)[b]	74	(32)[b]
Concealment could have caused death?	59	(85)[b]	54	(81)[b]
Accused was unwed?	70	(85)[b]	84	(81)[b]
Crime occurred in city (Boston, London)?	31	(95)[b]	63	(81)[b]
Victim was female?	47	(79)[b]	41	(92)[b]

[a] Frequency adjusted to omit missing data.

[b] Percentage of cases for which this information was available.

[c] In two cases, the victim was the illegitimate offspring of married women.

age of victim, and illegitimacy upon verdicts in Massachusetts, controlling for the interactive effects of all the variables, appears in Appendix 1.

There are some divergences within the large pattern of similarity in defendants and victims in 18th-century New England and English cases. Table 4.5 presents this data for the period between 1670 and 1780. By far the most common defendant was an unmarried mother of a newborn child. The deviations from this norm occur in the cells of the table showing the least comparability between Massachusetts and Middlesex, England. The first is the sex ratio. A difference exists between the percentage of female infants thought to be murdered in the two jurisdictions, which may be due to the small number of cases. In the light of the evidence from Chapter 5 that the sex ratio of victims was roughly one to one, this difference should be viewed as the result of too small a sample, although psychological reasons for male newborns suffering higher rates of neonaticide can be provided. These reasons revolve around the fact that the male child was the same sex as the absent father, and became a substitute for aggressions directed at the father.

More straightforward differences between the two jurisdictions lay in the defendants' relation to their victims, the defendants' occupations, and the scene of the crime. On the first subject: more death from casual contact, for example road accidents or the negligence of nurses and babysitters, in Middlesex, England, than in Massachusetts, is reflected in the court records. In metropolitan London, this was to be expected. In relatively rural Massachusetts, there was less danger from carts, and fewer nurses were employed. The variation in the occupation of the accused between England and New England—the largest divergence in the table—is directly proportional to the vast numbers of young people in positions of domestic servitude in England. This was unparalleled anywhere in Western Europe, including the Bay Colony. Finally, the disparity in urban setting of the crimes can be explained by the fact that London included one-third of the population of Middlesex, while Boston contained, for most of this period, less than one-tenth of the population of Massachusetts.[11]

The statistical picture of the defendant and her victim is constant over time and space, and the few extant anecdotal accounts of such women from the eighteenth-century sources give poignant substance to the statistical outline. In 1737, the *OBSP* included the report of a conversation between the ordinary of Newgate Prison and Sarah Allen, the latter awaiting execution for the murder of her newborn bastard. Allen was one of the few convicted on these charges in eighteenth-century England. The parson's tale of the penitent servant girl is familiar: Allen was a 27-year-old Buckinghamshire woman who had found a stable, respectable position as a servant in the city of London. She committed infanticide to avoid shame. The prison preacher reported that she rediscovered religion in the goal and died at peace with the world. In the contemporaneous Massachusetts case of Rebecca Chamblit, the plight of the defendant was similar. Atypically, both women had confessed to premeditation and suffered the full measure of the law. Because they were executed, their cases received public attention, and the historian gains a glimpse into their world. Save for their fate, they were typical of the accused.[12]

5

The Environmental Causes of Infanticide,
1558-1803

Frequency tables and cross-tabulations help the scholar to reconstruct the typical prisoner charged with infanticide and provide insights into the thinking of juries, but they cannot be used to explain variations in the number of cases from year to year. Across the broad expanse of two and a half centuries, the frequency of infanticide indictments varied greatly from year to year and period to period. Totals of prosecutions rose and fell under the influence of fluctuating patterns of economic and demographic growth, changing levels of stress and violence, and evolving social and cultural mores.

The student of infanticide in the sixteenth and seventeenth centuries deals with manifestations of social disorder: the population pressure, economic want, and the breakdown of social and community conventions discussed in the first chapter of this book. These travails were keenly felt among the poor, and broadly speaking, were motives for infanticide. Time series regression permits comparison of key economic, demographic, social, and emotional stress indicators with criminal indictments for the crime.

Examination of the external causes of crime in the eighteenth century requires a different frame of reference. Material improvements, increased life expectancy, and a rising standard of living, especially in the second half of the century, reflected themselves in a declining number of infanticide cases. In particular, the relative influence of medical and demographic changes upon infanticide can be more fully explored in the 1700s than for preceding centuries because of the greater volume of data available after 1700.

While mortality records in Tudor-Stuart England do not lend themselves readily to minute dissection, four large areas of possible environmental causation of infanticide do emerge. They are population pressure, scarcity of economic necessities, violence and stress in society, and widespread female disregard for sexual conventions.

The population of Elizabethan and Jacobean England was steadily rising, and it seems worthwhile to inquire whether, for the hard-pressed parent, infanticide may have been a form of birth control. In fact, it was not. For infanticide to lower population significantly, it must be directed at enough female infants to reduce the number of mothers who could bear children in the next generation. There is little evidence of imbalance in sex ratios of children in sixteenth and seventeenth century English parish registers, and there is little sex bias among the victims of infanticide in the court records. Between 1560 and 1603, there were 12 female neonates suspected of being murdered in Essex, and 13 male infants. Between 1603 and 1635, the comparable statistics for victims were 12 females and 12 males; from 1636 to 1650, nine females and eight males. For the whole of Hertfordshire, Sussex, and Middlesex, combined with London, between 1558 and 1624, the sex of infants whose deaths brought murder indictments was 43.9 percent male (61 cases) 41.7 percent female (58 cases) and 14.4 percent unrecorded. Moreover, the numbers of both sexes suspiciously dead, even if all the defendants were guilty of the charge, and three times as many went uncaught, was still too small to influence population growth.[1]

Of course, for infanticide to be a successful population

control mechanism in a country whose laws and legal officers regarded the act as murder, it must be condoned lo-
cally. Covert assent could have existed in isolated, tightly-
knit rural communities, poor urban subcultures like the
dockside parishes of London, or among bands of roving laborers. These groups might have assisted infanticidal parents or caretakers to conceal their crime. In the light of the
foregoing chapters, this kind of conspiracy appears to have
been rare. Local subversion of laws against illegitimacy can
be measured, and will be compared against infanticide indictment rates later in this chapter.

A more important demographic influence upon infanticide, albeit an indirect one, was the shortages created by the
increase of population in these years. The study of economic conditions offers a second perspective on the world
of the suspects and victims. Poverty was endemic in Tudor
and Stuart England, and the resulting exhaustion, starvation, and exposure were real threats to adult as well as child
life. Rising population, coupled with the squeezing of
poorer tenants off the land by enclosers and engrossers,
made food, heating, and building materials scarce for the
needy. In this period of steadily widening class distinctions,
landless, wandering laborers faced difficulty rearing families. Their lot was hard:

> . . . no lodging but the floor
> No stool to sit, no lock upon the door,
> No straw to make us litter in the night,
> Nor any candlesticks to hold the light.

With more sympathy than that shown by contemporary officials for the plight of the poor, the scholar may inquire
into the relationship between poverty and violence against
infants. For the poor female servant who could not afford
to lose her job, much less feed another mouth, just as for
the overburdened cottager family with perhaps one too
many offspring already, infanticide might have seemed a
matter of survival.[2]

Charitable benefactions to parishes and institutions for

Table 5.1
Infanticide and Charitable Benefactions
in the Home Counties, 1558–1624[a]

Period (Five year totals)	Infanticides	Charitable Benefactions (in 1000 £ units)
1558–1562	3	150
	9	120
	1	90
	11	95
	13	105
	15	110
	11	120
	12	125
	12	130
	8	165
	17	210
	30	350
1618–1622	9	425

[a]$R^2 = .59$, $b = .10$. Significant at the 85 percent level.

the care of the indigent were a dramatic private response to the rise of a class of wandering poor. The rate of these benefactions appears to have a relationship to the frequency of infanticide indictments. Regression of first differences of infanticide indictments with first differences of charitable benefactions revealed that the two events were closely related ($R^2 = .59$). (To avoid autocorrelation due to a common trend in both infanticide and charity time series, we regressed the increase or decrease from period to period—the first differences—for the two variables, rather than the raw data. This technique "detrends" the data.) If one views charity as an indication of the visibility of the misery of the poor, the increase in benefactions should correspond to an increase in crimes of desperation like infanticide. Of course, charity was not the cause of infanticide, but a simultaneous measure of the plight of the wandering poor. In effect, infanticide prosecutions and charitable gifts to the parishes for relief of the poor had the same prior cause—the dislocation of a large portion of society. In a narrower sense, the urge to give charity may have represented a merciful private obverse of the magistrates' public campaign against bastardy and vagrancy among the poor.

One must be wary of broader generalization because these results are greatly influenced by "outliers" on both chronological ends of data. The simultaneous peaking of indictments and benefactions in the last years of James I's reign is clear in Figure 5.1. Nevertheless, the connection between indictments for infanticide and private recognition of the plight of the poor suggests that economic deprivation had some role in the rise and fall of criminal prosecutions.[3]

In an attempt to identify the relative causal importance of more precise economic factors, the authors have compared five-year totals of infanticide indictments with grain prices, real wages for agricultural laborers, and timber prices. Raw figures are presented in Table 5.2. The infan-

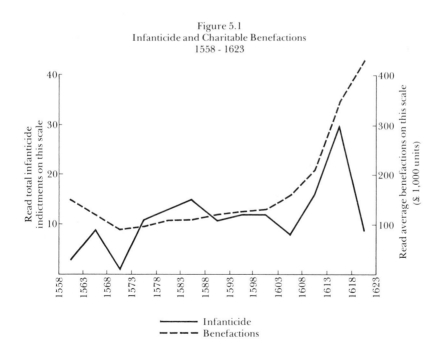

Figure 5.1
Infanticide and Charitable Benefactions
1558 - 1623

——— Infanticide
- - - - Benefactions

Table 5.2
Economic Need and Infanticide
in the Home Counties, 1558–1624[a]

| Period | Infanticide (five-year totals) | | | | | Prices (five-year averages) | | Real Wages for Agricultural Laborers[d] (by decades) |
	Middlesex	Essex	Herts	Sussex	Total	Grains[b]	Timber[c]	
1558–	no data	1	no data	2	3	321	178	
1563–	1	5	no data	3	9	305	182	59
1568–	0	1	no data	0	1	321	197	
1573–	2	4	1	4	11	388	210	66
1578–	3	7	0	3	13	417	226	
1583–	2	11	2	0	15	460	253	60
1588–	1	4	1	5	11	460	258	
1593–	2	5	1	4	12	694	296	57
1598–	2	6	2	2	12	576	308	
1603–	5	3	0	0	8	502	334	49
1608–	7	6	1	3	17	655	368	
1613–	21	4	2	3	30	688	392	50
1618–	no data[e]	3	2	4	9	598	455	

[a]For prices and wages, 1450–1499 = 100.
[b]Grain prices, $R^2 = .14$, $b = .02$.
[c]Timber prices, $R^2 = .38$; $b = .13$. Significant at 90 percent level.
[d]Real wage, $R = .11$, $b = .22$.
[e]This excludes one case from January 1618, see Table 5.3.

ticide cases in this computation included presentments by the coroner's inquest, as well as true bills at the assizes. Comparisons of infanticide with economic and social statistics are best served by the broadest definition of infanticide cases. The four counties selected circle the city of London and its suburbs. They are the counties for which the earliest criminal statistics are available and for which contemporaneous price and wage indices taken from London markets are most applicable. The first necessity of life is food, and the poor population lived on bread. If they were lucky, it was wheat bread, but more often than not it was barley, oat, rye, or other grains mixed with peas. Grain prices measure the cost of this staple. Timber was a necessity for heating and for lodging. Real wages for agricultural laborers has obvious relevance when so many potential infanticidal parents fit this category.[4]

The results of regression of infanticide in the home circuit counties of Hertford, Essex, and Sussex, and the county of Middlesex with food prices and real wages indicated that economic want did not play a major direct role in causing infanticide. In view of the large number of poor who did not destroy their children, this conclusion seems sensible. A relationship does exist between timber prices and infanticide indictments. Changes in the price of wood explain 38 percent of the fluctuation in prosecution of infanticide ($R^2 = .38$). Only ten times out of a hundred would this result occur without a real relationship between the crime and the timber price index (a 90 percent significance level). Wood provided shelter and fuel for parents and children, and Elizabethan and Jacobean England was in the throes of a critical timber shortage. Exposure of a newborn baby (whose body heat control mechanisms are not developed until many months after birth) on a cold floor could very shortly result in death. If the neglect was premeditated, the exposure was murder. Cases of this type, though rare, were tried at the assizes.

Food prices might have been expected to measure a parallel causal process to timber prices—deprivation of parents'

caloric intake, resulting in starvation of unwanted infants—
but the grain price index does not show a high correlation
with infanticide statistics. Exposure may simply have been a
more effective means of causing death than starvation. Perhaps deliberate exposure was easier for neighbors and coroners to detect than deliberate starvation. One may also surmise that long-term grain price fluctuations were more
sensitive to manipulation by speculators than were timber
prices. The further removed the price index was from local
conditions, the less accurate an indicator of local distress it
would be. Declines in real wage levels also do not seem to
have been a cause of infanticidal behavior, perhaps because
the laborers included in the computations were primarily
men and perpetrators of infanticide were women.

If economic factors did not have a direct impact upon the
rate of infanticide, perhaps their effect was indirect, flowing
through the rising general levels of violence and stress.
(On the indirect impact see Appendix 3.) Deprivation and
want is a prime cause of stress. Stress, violence, and sexual
deviance were linked together in Tudor-Stuart England.
Murder, manslaughter, and assault were common, as duell-
ists, gangs, and highwaymen took out their frustrations on
each other and innocent bystanders. Major legislation
against fornicators, drinkers, swearers, non-churchgoers,
parents of bastards, and alehouse-keepers, enacted in Elizabeth I's and James I's reigns, increased the level of stress
in the society, that is, the gap between official norms and
standards and individual needs and customs. Men and
women on the margins of society, including the wandering
poor, were particularly susceptible to this stress. Increased
stress led to anger and violence. As the level of stress in the
society varied, so varied the potential for violent crimes
against oneself and others.

Raoul Naroll, a cultural anthropologist, has devised a
general index of stress applicable to historical situations.
The index includes murder, witchcraft, suicide, and alcoholism. The former two offenses reflect aggressive exter-
nalizations of stress; the second two are equally violent in-
ternalizations of stress. To the aggressive stress indicators,

Table 5.3
Infanticide and Aggressive Stress in Middlesex, 1613–1618
(Female Defendants in Parentheses)

Period (six months)	Infanticide	Murder and Manslaughter [a] (of adults only)	Rape [b]	Assault [c]	Witchcraft [d]
March 1613–	1 (1)	4 (2)	4 (0)	45 (8)	0 (0)
September 1613–	4 (3)	7 (0)	2 (0)	29 (7)	4 (3)
March 1614–	4 (3)	10 (1)	6 (0)	36 (11)	4 (3)
September 1614–	3 (2)	4 (1)	3 (0)	33 (6)	1 (1)
March 1615–	1 (1)	3 (0)	0 (0)	34 (4)	1 (1)
September 1615–	1 (1)	10 (1)	1 (0)	63 (10)	0 (0)
March 1616–	3 (3)	8 (1)	0 (0)	53 (10)	2 (2)
September 1616–	1 (1)	7 (1)	2 (0)	40 (9)	1 (1)
March 1617–	2 (2)	4 (2)	0 (0)	33 (3)	1 (1)
September 1617–	2 (1)	6 (0)	1 (0)	40 (11)	2 (1)

(Column header: *Aggressive Stress* spans Murder and Manslaughter, Rape, Assault, Witchcraft)

[a] $R^2 = .11$, $b = .70$.
[b] $R^2 = .14$, $b = .60$.
[c] $R^2 = .17$, $b = .05$.
[d] $R^2 = .76$, $b = .75$, significant at 99 percent level.
Although manslaughter had become a separate crime under the law, in aggressive terms its results were the same as murder: a mortal assault. In addition, indictments for murder were reduced to convictions for manslaughter fairly often.

one may add rape and assault. With the internal stress indicators, for reasons discussed momentarily, belongs prostitution. Study of these manifestations of the strain of life illuminate the extent to which external conditions induced individuals to do violence to infants.[5]

To utilize the full battery of stress indicators, the authors sought well populated jurisdictions. The first of these was urban greater London, between 1613 and 1618. Confinement to this period avoids the great plague years of 1603 and 1625. During the period between 1613 and 1618 the population was expanding at a steady rate of about 8000 immigrants a year, and prices and wages were fairly uniform. The result of simple regression of indicators of aggressive stress with infanticide appears in Table 5.3. Rape and assault, men's crimes, showed no relation to infanticide, suggesting that the best measures of the effect of aggressive

stress upon infanticide cases would be those most closely
linked to women. Witchcraft, which fits this prescription,
does show a strong relationship to infanticide. Chapters 1
and 2 explored this association. The connection between infanticide and other homicides is complex, and requires
more attention.[6]

The correlation of infanticide with murder and manslaughter of adults, crimes which had the same legal definition, is small. Changes in the frequency of murder and
manslaughter explain only 11 percent of the variation in
infanticide indictments. (The figures given above for infanticide cases in both Middlesex and Essex represent only true
bills for the crimes. Reports and suspicions of the crime,
reflected in coroner's inquests, are not appropriate measures of actual aggressive acts.) Infanticide involved more
planning than manslaughter, which by definition was a
crime without premeditation. The murder of another adult
did not, perhaps, call forth the same emotions as the deliberate killing of a child. Metropolitan London had more
than its share of death by duels and gang-fighting, which
may have obscured any underlying relationship between
murder and infanticide.

Against this last possibility, comparison of murder and infanticide in the rural precincts of Essex acts as a check. The
two crimes are very weakly related to one another, at least
insofar as their appearance in the courtroom is a measure
of their actual occurrance.[7] Bearing in mind that the absence of records for a number of assize court sittings might
change these findings, a "corrected" table for the indictments one might expect to find in the missing sittings was
created. This table served as a basis for a second comparison of murder and manslaughter with infanticide. (See Appendix 2.) In fact, the correction for missing data increased
the amount of variation in infanticide that murder explained, to 21.8 percent ($R^2 = .218$). This is a material but
small change. Assize records from Sussex show similar small
relationships between changes in numbers of murder and
manslaughter cases in the years under study and the rate of

Table 5.4
Aggressive Stress in Essex, 1560–1647[a]

Period (four year totals)	Infanticide	Murder and Manslaughter (adult victims only)
1560–1563	3	8
1564	4	7
1568	2	8
1572	1	6
1576	3	14
1580	5	25
1584	4	14
1588	4	25
1592	3	22
1596	2	12
1600	3	32
1604	insufficient data[b]	
1608	6	22
1612	2	9
1616	3	11
1620	3	5
1624	6	13
1628	9	15
1632	6	8
1636	4	4
1640	3	7
1644	7	7

[a] $R^2 = .15$, $b = .37$. Significant at the 75 percent level.
[b] Too few assize sittings have been preserved to provide data.

infanticide. For three-year intervals from 1559 to 1600, Sussex infanticide and adult murder-manslaughter indictments covaried with an $R^2 = .133$ and a slope $= .141$.

There is an important fact about the ages of victims to be learned from these tabulations. Children were victims in about 30 percent of all murder indictments in Essex; 34 percent of all murder indictments in Middlesex, and 28 of all murder indictments in Sussex. This is not surprising in one sense, for the proportion of the population under the age of nine in these counties was probably between 33 and

50 percent of the total. The risk to suffer infanticide sharply declined as a child grew older; 80 percent of the cases involved neonate victims. Newborn children did not comprise 25 percent of the population, and so they suffered this crime in numbers that far outweighed their numbers in the population. Infants born in Tudor and Stuart times were likely to suffer murder in far greater proportions to adults than later generations of children. Infanticide was but 10 percent of all murder indictments in eighteenth-century Middlesex, and but 2 percent of the cases of murder and manslaughter brought to trial in England and Wales between 1960 and 1970. While the absolute numbers of infanticide cases slightly increased over the centuries, the proportion of aggressive stress expressed as infanticide was far greater in early modern England than in later years. The fact that children suffered the externalization of aggression of their elders, in particular their parents, in rough proportion to their number in the population, suggests that they had no special status in early modern England. Evidence from court records, manuals, letters, and diaries about the harsh disciplining of children, the often brutal treatment of servants and apprentices, and the deaths of children through beating confirms this surmise.[8]

The internalization of stress may be partly responsible for the weak correlation between infanticide and external aggressive stress crimes. The two parts of the stress measurement battery are not duplicative, but opposite. Studies on the inverse relationship between murder and suicide by Porterfield and by Henry and Short reveal a basic division in stress relief strategies. Violence may be directed either at others or at oneself, but only a few individuals characteristically do both. A recent investigation of suicide and murder in Houston, Texas, concluded that the two crimes are "polar opposites." Aggressive and introjective stress, drawing upon different psychological sources, may be additive measures of stress in a society.[9]

Among forms of introjected stress, suicide, alcoholism, and prostitution were certainly familiar to Elizabethan and

Jacobean authorities. Suicide is not a byproduct of industrial modernity. Elizabethans William Shakespeare dwelt upon self-destruction, and Christopher Marlowe seemed bent upon it. Anxiety and depression then, as today, could result in the violent internalization of pain. Drinking to excess is also a form of withdrawal from reality resting upon self-abuse. In both bustling London and bucolic Essex, few sessions of the courts passed without cases of drunk and disorderly conduct. Prostitution was, in some sense, normal, for it has been practiced throughout history for economic gain. From a different perspective, however, prostitution was regarded as a degrading form of behavior in Tudor-Stuart England. "Whore" and "prostitute" were words of opprobrium, even when hurled by women of ill-repute at each other. For many women, the origin of prostitution lies in self-dislike and the desire to be punished, and "prostitution fantasies" involve subjugation and masochism.[10]

Overtly, infanticide is a form of aggressive behavior, but modern psychiatric studies have discovered that the crime has a decided introjective component as well. (These categories of motivation are traced more fully in Chapter 6.) The three introjective stress measures introduced above touch upon distinct aspects of the psychology of infanticidal parents. The first, suicide, is often the goal of "altruistic suicide" murders of young children by their parents. Situational stress disorders, frequently associated with drinking, account for another portion of modern infanticides. The same depression that leads to alcoholism may in other circumstances induce infanticide. Other infanticidal parents with character disorders murder children with indifference. Today, these women are found to have long records of moral violations, including prostitution.[11] Comparison of measures of introjective stress with infanticide offer both promising and disappointing results.

Women as well as men drank, but only the male public-nuisance drinker who abused the constables, threatened people in the streets, or was a common offender was arrested for the crime, with the result that there was little cor-

Table 5.5
Infanticide and
Introjective Stress in Middlesex, 1613–1618
(indicates crime by women)

| Period | Infanticide | Introjective Stress | | |
		Prostitution[a]	Drink[b]	Suicide
March 1613–	1 (1)	12 (all)	8	none listed
	4 (3)	11 (all)	6	none listed
	4 (3)	8 (all)	8 (1)	none listed
	3 (2)	10 (all)	3 (1)	none listed
	1 (1)	1 (all)	3	none listed
	1 (1)	2 (all)	6	none listed
	3 (3)	7 (all)	4	none listed
	1 (1)	0	1	none listed
	2 (2)	1 (all)	3	none listed
September 1617– March 1618	2 (1)	0	3	none listed

[a] $R^2 = .30, b = .14.$
[b] $R^2 = .09, b = .16.$

relation of infanticide with drinking. Suicide, which is a reliable indicator of introjective stress in the latter portions of the eighteenth century, occurred in seventeenth-century London, but was rarely recorded as such. It was greatly under recorded because if this cause of death was given the victim could not be buried in holy ground. The last indicator, prostitution, works fairly well. This is an encouraging fact, for prostitution charges were confined to women and involved the very sort of sexual license which magistrates ascribed to infanticide suspects.[12]

The relationship between infanticide and prostitution opens a wider avenue of inquiry into the environmental causes of infanticide in Tudor-Stuart England. Economic distress and emotional strain may have led poorer women to disregard or even defy official pronouncements on sexual conduct. Refusal to accept the normative sexual prescriptions of a culture—asocialization—may have been reflected in premarital copulation and lewd conduct among women. These actions struck at the heart of the domestic catechism taught women by clergymen and handbook authors. "Gentility, inoffensiveness, and passivity" were joined in these lessons with moral self-discipline. Above all, the young woman was to avoid the temptations of the flesh. If infanticide were actually a form of defiance of sexual norms, the volume of infanticide cases should vary positively with other incidences of sexual offenses.[13]

Illegitimacy is the broadest indicator of disregard for conventional sexual conduct. It may be traced through study of parish birth records. In early Stuart England, about 20 percent of all first births occurred before nine months had passed in marriage. If infanticide were one common way of disposing of the unwanted results of illegitimate unions, in effect an extension of the sexual offense, the rate of illegitimacy would be closely tied to the rate of infanticide. Spillover of infanticides into the courts would vary in size with the extent to which illegitimacies occurred. If communities conspired with infanticidal parents to cover up the crimes, this comparison would be invalid, but after the poor laws of 1576 and the succeeding years' prosecution of infanticide suspects, such conspiracies do not seem probable. If an actual increase in the commission of infanticide was linked to an increase in illegitimacy, and this in turn caused the rising numbers of cases in the courts, a strong correlation should exist between illegitimacy and infanticide. A high positive relationship of this type would cast doubt upon the argument in Chapter 1, to wit, that the rise in prosecutions was as much created by growing magisterial interest and efficiency in ferreting out the crime, as by an increase in actual offenses.

Peter Laslett and Karla Osterveen have estimated the illegitimacy rate for English counties from parish records. Their estimate is compared with total infanticide prosecutions for the period between 1558 and 1624 in Table 5.6. Suspected cases of infanticide are included in this total, in addition to the smaller number of true bills at the assizes. We limit ourselves to the years before 21 James I, c. 27 to avoid the complications of the inflation of indictments by the infanticide statute. The positive slope ($b = 2.62$) indicates that as illegitimacy rose, infanticide increased two and one-half times as rapidly. This relationship would require complicated explication were it not rendered nugatory by the very weak correlation between the two offenses. Illegitimacy explained but 13.2 percent of variation in infanticide indictments ($R^2 = .132$).[14]

Table 5.6
Illegitimacy and Infanticide
in the Home Counties and Middlesex, 1558–1624[a]

Infanticide in Five-year Totals (Essex, Middlesex, Herts, Sussex)		Illegitimacy as percent of Registered Births
1558–	3	1.6
1563–	9	1.9
1568–	1	2.4
1573–	11	3.2
1578–	13	3.4
1583–	15	4.1
1588–	11	4.7
1593–	12	4.5
1598–	12	4.4
1603–	8	4.0
1608–	17	3.5
1613–	30	3.3
1618–	9	3.1

[a]$R^2 = .132$, $b = 2.62$. Regression statistics computed for this book.

David Levine and Keith Wrightson have explored one reason why illegitimacy might not have led to infanticide. In their study of the social context of illegitimacy in the parish of Terling, Essex, they establish the fact that illegitimacy was not intended as deviance, but was instead a part of a larger pattern of acceptable social behavior. Their figures (see Table 5.7) are close to those of Laslett and Osterveen, though the correlation between infanticide and illegitimacy one calculates from Levine and Wrightson's data is smaller

Table 5.7
Illegitimacy and Infanticide in Essex, 1558–1624[a]

Period	Infanticide in Five-year Totals (All Essex)	Illegitimacy as Percent of Registered Births (Terling, Essex)[b]
1558–	1	1.0
	5	1.9
	1	2.5
	4	2.1
	7	1.9
	11	3.5
	4	6.0
	5	7.9
	6	9.3
	3	8.0
	6	6.0
	4	4.5
1618–	3	3.0

[a] $R^2 = .025$, $b = .152$. Regression statistics computed for this book.
[b] The implicit assumption here is that Terling parish was in this respect "typical" of Essex.

than that in Table 5.6. Using Levine and Wrightson's figures, one finds that illegitimacy explains but 2.5 percent of the fluctuation in infanticide cases. Their description of illegitimate unions, while not directed to the issue of infanticide, does explain the low correlation. The peak of illegitimacy, which Laslett and Osterveen uncover for all England, and Levine and Wrightson validate in their parish, was the result of two events. One was conventional and accepted, the other unexpected and disconcerting for the young people involved. It was customary for young men and women who were more or less engaged to sleep together, with the understanding that they would marry eventually, or sooner if a pregnancy resulted from their lovemaking. The crop failures of 1590s made such marriages impossible, but did not at first deter young people from their amours. The sudden increase in illegitimacy in those years did not bespeak a wave of disrespect for sexual controls, but merely the inability of the young to adapt quickly enough to the realities of their world. The rise in infanticide and recorded illegitimacy coincided somewhat because both shared as one root cause the economic conditions of the 1590s. The relationship between the two offenses over the long span of time was weak—despite the large numbers of bastard infanticide victims—because magistrates continued to seek out and find infanticide long after the great mass of young couples had adjused their sexual habits to economic necessity.[15]

By the mid-1610s, the increase in illegitimacy was beginning to subside. Bastardy was nevertheless still punishable under the poor laws, and men and women who flouted the 1576 and 1609 statutes regularly faced justice at the quarter sessions courts. These cases, unlike the illegitimacy recovered from parish records, reflected magisterial enforcement of sexual norms. If the direct effect of official labelling of sexual deviance upon infanticide indictment rates propounded in Chapter 1 is correct, bastardy cases and infanticide cases should be more closely linked than infanticide and illegitimacy. This was so in Jacobean Middlesex. From Middlesex quarter sessions records, one finds that fluctuations in bastardy cases explain 34 percent of the

Table 5.8
Criminal Bastardy and Infanticide in Middlesex, 1613–1618[a]

Period (six months)	Infanticide	Bastardy
March 1613–	1	11
September 1613	4	22
March 1614–	4	21
September 1614–	3	15
March 1615–	1	9
September 1615–	1	17
March 1616–	3	7
September 1616–	1	3
March 1617–	2	10
September 1617–	2	19

[a]$R^2 = .343$, $b = .113$. Significant at the 90 percent level.

changes in infanticide indictments. The effect of the former on the latter is small and positive; for each new case of bastardy, there was but .113 new cases of infanticide. Magistrates found the two offenses rising and falling together.

In Essex, the relationship between bastardy investigations and infanticide cases was not quiet as strong as in Middlesex, and was inverse in direction. (The Pearson correlation coefficient (r) for this regression = −.449, fairly strong and negative.) As punishments for bastardy were increasingly meted out, arrests for infanticide declined. Bastardy explains 20 percent of the rise and fall of infanticide. An increase of one bastardy case resulted in a decrease of .056 infanticides. (When corrected for missing quarter sessions records, the relationship between bastardy and infanticide in Essex does not change materially. Common variation (R^2) declined to about 16 percent. The slope of the relationship (*b*) rose to about −.128, meaning that an increase of one bastardy case led to a .128 decline in infanticide cases. This is far closer in shape to the causal relationship in Middlesex, albeit with the opposite sign. The effect of bastardy upon infanticide in the two jurisdictions was similar in pattern, though inverse in outcome. The full table for the corrected comparison appears in Appendix 2.) In Essex, more than Middlesex, every time a bastard pregnancy was exposed, the possibility for the prospective mother to hide her condition and later to conceal murder of the child decreased. Social control of this type worked in Essex, and not in Middlesex. To escape the vigilance of the justices of the peace and knowing neighbors, an unwed pregnant woman might well flee the country and turn her steps toward London. This may explain why the slope of the relationship between bastardy and infanticide in the metropolis was positive. Magistates simply could not monitor the immorality of the poor in teeming London as well as in rural Essex.

If infanticide was caused by female indifference to sexual continence, the correlation between bastardy cases and infanticide cases—given the vast majority of bastards among the victims—should be very much larger than the figures

Table 5.9
Bastardy and Infanticide in Essex, 1576–1619[a]

Period[b]	Infanticide	Bastardy
1576–1579	3	16
1580	5	13
1584	4	16
1588	4	20
1592	3	15
1596	2	23
1600	3	42
1604	insufficient data	
1608	6	21
1612	2	36
1616	3	35

[a]$R^2 = .201$, $b = .056$. Significant at the 90 percent level.

[b]Four year periods are used in this table instead of five year periods, in order to get at least ten intervals for comparison between 1576 and 1623. Bastardy convictions begin with the poor law of 1576, and infanticide totals are effected by the 1624 statute, so the comparison had to be confined within the period above. The reduction to four-year intervals does not endanger the validity of regression techniques.

actually discovered. The conclusion is clear: Infanticide was not caused by nor was it a part of female defiance against sexual constraints. A last expression of asocialization, lewd behavior, validates the conclusion above. With prostitution and bastardy cases omitted, sexual offenses run the gamut from lewd carriage, wanton dalliance, and promiscuity, to keeping and frequenting bawdy houses. Compared with all of these sex offenses, infanticide in Middlesex between 1612 and 1618 show no real relationship ($R^2 = .01$). The lack of association again suggests that infanticide was not meant as a violation or an attack upon sexual standards. Lewdness, like bastardy, did not of itself lead to violence against infants. Infanticide was not an extension of actual female immorality, though magistrates and lawmakers in this age thought differently.

Late sixteenth- and early seventeenth-century infanticide was a product of violent emotions in a violent age. The potential for killing one's own infants was affected by economic conditions and indifference to moral codes, although these forces spent their power indirectly, through the level of stress and aggressive violence of the society. Multiple regressions of all these variables with infanticide show that, while economic want and sexual immorality had some small direct influence upon the rate of infanticide prosecution, the former two conditions did have powerful effects upon aggressive and introjective stress, and thereby, indirect effect upon the crime. The combined direct and indirect effect of all the environmental causes discussed above explained 87 percent (multiple $R^2 = .87$) of the variation in infanticide cases brought to the Elizabethan and Jacobean courts. (In Appendix 3, a "path analysis" of these relationships is provided.)

One anticipates that improved material conditions would directly and indirectly reduce the number of infanticides. Using eighteenth-century demographic, medical, and economic sources for England and New England, one can test this proposition. Material improvement changed Anglo-American society in a number of ways, two of which are of prime importance in the study of infanticide. Mortality rates declined and times of famine grew infrequent. To be sure, infant death and maternal death in childbirth remained common, and single cases of starvation occurred often enough, but only rarely were entire regions overwhelmed by these perils. In ascending order of specificity, measures of demographic and economic change will be compared with infanticide indictments. The analysis will proceed from the general mortality rate, the suicide rate, the age-specific infant death rate, the stillbirth rate, the rate of mothers dying in childbirth, to the rate at which infants were "accidentally" overlaid, and then turn to the effects of food and coal prices and wages upon infanticide, seeking the connection between external conditions and the frequency of indictments.

In her classic essay on life in eighteenth-century London, Dorothy George proposed a simple yardstick to measure the quality of life: "the test of change [in the quality of life] is the death rate, which begins to fall after 1750, and falls more rapidly after 1780." The death rate for greater London in the three periods between 1702 and 1750, 1751 and 1780, and 1781 and 1800 was 48.8 per thousand, 43.4 per thousand, and 35.1 per thousand, respectively. General English mortality in the same periods was 32.7, 30.5 and 27.8 per thousand per year. Although the combined 50-year rate for the period between 1700 and 1750 hides a jump in mortality between 1720 and 1750, wherever one looks in the realm the gross downward trend over the century is clear. Declining mortality meant rising life expectancy. As life expectancy for parents increased, the lot of childbearers must have improved. This improvement matched the overall decline in infanticide indictments. While this general relationship fits the hypothesis, specific quantitative measures of the effect of demographic changes upon infanticide must still be tested.[16]

Within the statistics of mortality, suicide provides a first, dramatic estimate of subjective human response to deprivation and scarcity. While suicide was not as important a contributor to eighteenth-century mortality as epidemic diseases and poor harvests, the suicide rate was responsive to hard times. "Bills of Mortality" recorded cases of suicide for eighteenth-century London over much the same area as that covered by the king's justices for London and Middlesex, permitting comparison of suicide statistics with infanticide indictments. To remove the effects of yearly changes in mortality rates for greater London, it is necessary to compute the "rate" of suicide. The suicide rate used here is the number of reported suicides divided by the number of deaths recorded in that year. Regression of the suicide rate upon infanticide indictments for the early part of the century, from 1707 to 1727, showed that suicide explained 27.5 percent of the variation in infanticide cases ($R^2 = .275$, at a significance level of 80 percent). Similarly, in regression of suicide rates upon infanticide between 1764 and 1784, the suicide rate changes explained 23.9 percent of infanticides

($R^2 = .239$, at a significance level of 80 percent). The slopes of the relationships between infanticide and suicide rate for the two periods were -4451 and $+3812$ respectively. In the early years of the century, the -4451 slope implies that infanticide rates decreased 4451 times for each one unit rise in the suicide rate. This inverse relationship is spurious. Suicide was being reported to the keepers of the bills for the first time in anything close to its true numbers. (In Appendix 5, yearly totals for all categories of the Bill of Mortality used in this chapter are reported.) The leap in the number of suicides admitted to authorities with each passing year artificially inflated these statistics. More stock should be placed in the finding that, in the late portions of the century, suicide and infanticide indictments were falling together. This finding, along with data on infant death rates and food prices presented later in this chapter, confirms that the "quality of life" thesis works far better for the second half of the eighteenth century than for its opening years. Dorothy George reached the same conclusion. The association between infanticide and suicide is strong enough to use the latter as a measure of introjective stress, but not clear enough to prove suicidal impulses a major cause of infanticide. (Multiple regression of environmental forces upon infanticide, leading to a path analysis of the ordering of eighteenth-century causes, appears in Appendix 3.) [17]

Suicide is a measure of the generalized perception of the quality of life. It is not specific to those particularly at risk to suffer or to commit infanticide. The applications of George's yardstick to the latter subject requires age and sex specific mortality rates. In London, the recorded infant mortality rate for those up to five years of age fell from 70 per hundred live births at the beginning of the century to 30 per hundred at its close. The fact that registration of very young infants' deaths in parish records was not reliable raises these figures, but such a correction would not change the downward course of infant mortality. For the same years, in Colyton, Devonshire, raw infant mortality for those up to a year old fell from 9.18 per hundred live births at the opening of the century to 7.2 per hundred at its end. In those North Shropshire parishes with good burial records, about 20 of 100 live births ended in death before the age of one year, between 1660 and 1710. By the middle of the eighteenth century, this figure had fallen to 16 or 17 per hundred live births, and fell still further to 13 per hundred by the close of the century. In Nottingham, comparable statistics for 1700, 1750, and 1800 are 17.9, 17.4, and 17.3 deaths for infants up to a year old per hundred live births. These figures support the general thesis, for they decline as infanticide declines. The causal relationship between infant death and infanticide can nevertheless be more closely traced.[18]

It is difficult to analyze the actual causes of infant death in these years because of the primitiveness of the descriptions in the London Bills of Mortality. For example, "colick" and "convulsions," commonly assigned causes of infant mortality, were symptoms, not causes of death. Nevertheless, for the first part of the century, the bills do render a yearly total of children who died before the age of six months. Infant death, during the months before weaning, when a mother's breast feeding gave her immunities to the child, might reflect some degree of neglect or impoverishment. Dividing the number of children who died before the age of six months by the total number of burials creates a rate of infant death, averages of which can be regressed against totals of infanticide indictments from the *OBSP*. The resulting infant death rate explains 33.9 percent of the variation in infanticide ($R^2 = .339$, with significance at the 85 percent level). The slope of this relationship, the b coefficient, was -3450. The negative slope indicates an inverse relationship; in this case, as the death rate of infants up to six months old increased, the infanticide rate declined. It is possible that the mortality of so many infants made the survivors all the more precious, but it is more probable that the result is a byproduct of a different process. The years between 1707 and 1727 were very unhealthy ones for the city of London, and the tremendous increase of infant mortality there from epidemic disease may have served to conceal infanticides from the eyes of neighbors and magistrates.

A comparison of infanticide and infant mortality taken from the bills for children up to two years old from 1764 to 1787 is more reliable. The geographic area they covered had been expanded, and the numbers seem more appropriate for the mortality of children in that era. This comparison sustains—albeit weakly—the quality of life thesis. Extension of the age of the child to two years introduces the probability that the infant death rate will be heavily influenced by epidemic diseases. Nevertheless, by comparing averages of infant death rates with infanticide indictment totals, one learns that the former explains 17.9 percent of the change in the latter ($R^2 = .179$, significant at the 80 percent level). The slope of this relationship is 46, illustrating the positive relationship between declining infant mortality and the unlikelihood of infanticide.

One may skirt the unreliability of infant death statistics by restricting attention to the child born dead, the child who was overlaid (smothered in bed) "accidentally" by its parents, and the mother who died in childbirth or directly afterwards. All three forms of mortality reflect the resources that parents and social institutions allocated to the health of infants. Edward Shorter believes that a mother's love for the forthcoming child had a large part in determining whether it would live, and wonders what steps a mother might have taken "at [her] own initiative, to minimize the loss" of life which delivery and early child care meant to her. In earlier centuries, child death sometimes resulted from deliberate neglect of the child after delivery. The extent to which mothers let this occur serves to measure maternal attachment to newborns. David Hunt portrays one such neglectful mother: "I picture a mother, who herself probably did not get enough to eat, and who was forced to work long and difficult hours, turning to the task of breast-feeding with mixed feelings. The child was a parasite; he did nothing and yet his appetites seemed to be endless." One solution was to turn the child over to wet-nurses, and the proportion of these unfortunate infants on the continent who died before their first year was well over half. Wet-nursing was never very common in England, however.[19]

Using the London bills and the *OBSP* one can compare the number of infanticide indictments with the number of children reported dead at birth or within a short time of it. A stillborn rate is prepared by dividing the stillborn by the number of successful births (from baptisms) plus the number of stillbirths. Comparison of the stillbirth rate and infanticide cases for the period between 1707 and 1727 showed a covariance of only 16 percent ($R^2 = .161$), and for the period from 1764 to 1784, a common variation of 8 percent ($R^2 = .080$). (Three-year averages of stillbirth rates were regressed upon three-year totals of infanticide.) These results are very weak, in part perhaps because deaths during and immediately after delivery often occurred despite the mother's intentions, whatever they may have been.

A variation on Shorter's theory is to compare the number of infants dead from "overlaying," supposedly accidental smothering of an infant in bed with its parents, recorded in the London bills, with the number of indictments (not including overlaying) for infanticide in the Middlesex English courts. Even a truly "accidental" overlaying showed a domestic arrangement with little provision for the safety, much less the comfort, of infants. For the years between 1707 and 1727, overlaying explained 26.1 percent of the variation in infanticide ($R^2 = .261$ at 80 percent significance level). (Three-year totals of overlaying were regressed with three-year totals of infanticide.) The later years from 1764 to 1787 saw a decrease of overlaying to low levels, two and three per year, numbers that explained 25.2 percent of the fluctuations in infanticide ($R^2 = .252$, significance level of 80 percent). The slopes of the relationships for the early and late eighteenth century were .152 and .388, respectively, showing the small positive effect of asocialization, as measured by overlaying, upon infanticide. The quality of life thesis is again confirmed (conceding the possible mislabelling of some "crib deaths," sudden infant death syndrome, as overlaying).

A third revision of Shorter's general approach turns attention to the mother's survival. Shorter found that within specific national or regional Western European value systems, the socioeconomic status of the parents did not correlate well with the survival rate of their infants. He concluded that the attention given to childbearing in a society outweighed family wealth in determining the rate at which children would live or die. This result directs scholars to examine the social importance assigned to childrearing in a culture, rather than simply measuring infant mortality. If a poor mother feels real affection for her offspring but is forced to work until the arrival of labor pains, refused adequate medical aid, and offered no assistance, her infant will suffer whatever her intentions may be. The rate of maternal death in childbed and from post partum diseases measures the value that society gives to mothering. This calculation avoids the contamination of infant mortality and stillborn rates by covert birth-control infanticides. While the latter were not widespread, cases of infanticide still passed as accidental or epidemic deaths. From the bills for greater London, a childbed death rate for women can be computed by dividing the number of mothers who died giving birth or shortly thereafter from birth-related causes, by the number of such deaths plus the number of successful births. When the childbed mortality rate is compared with infanticide indictments from the OBSP for the years between 1707 and 1727, one finds a covariance of approximately zero ($R^2 = .048$). For the period from 1764 to 1784 the covariance is larger, but not great ($R^2 = .154$). The degree of support society gave to the childbearing enterprise did not influence potential infanticidal mothers very much, though some effect was visible in the second half of the century.[20]

While statistics show some inverse relationship between improving infant and maternal conditions and infanticide indictment rates—as the health and welfare of mothers and children improved infanticide declined—all of the correlations lack great strength. The weakness of the correlation is due to the fact that progress in the care of infants and the lot of mothers was not as marked among the very poor of London—the most likely perpetrators of the crime—as upon the wealthier mothers of the city and the surrounding countryside. The London Foundling Hospital, opened in 1741 to care for infants abandoned by the poor in the city, along with its parliamentary-sponsored cousins in the provinces after 1756, became places of death for the infants of the very poor. Whether these establishments reduced the numbers of infanticides by providing an alternative to the crime, or effectually increased it, by making it easier for a destitute mother to avoid rearing her own child, cannot be determined. Nevertheless, the creation of government institutions for the care of poor infants, instead of increased prosecution of those suspected of doing away with their offspring, may be regarded as a sign of growing official sympathy to the plight of the poor mother and her infant. The numbers of very young children given to the institutions for care, some with notes from parents promising to return for the child when the family situation had improved, might represent not an alternative form of infanticide, but an alternative to neglect and eventual death for the infant within poor families or single parent families. If this is true, then the overcrowding of the foundling hospitals is evidence of increasing maternal sentiment—which, when viewed in conjunction with the declining infanticide indictment rate, suggests that the dark figure of infanticide might have been decreasing as material conditions and hope for the future progressed.[21]

The second broad measure of quality of life relevant to the study of infanticide is the availability of subsistence—food, shelter, and wages to purchase other necessities. For London and its surrounding countryside, changes in wheat and coal prices and real wages of laborers have been compiled, which may be compared with infanticide indictments in the *OBSP*. (Three-year averages of price and wage indices were regressed upon three-year infanticide totals. No detrending was necessary when comparing the variables within the periods from 1707 to 1727 and 1764 to 1784.) Changes in coal and wheat prices and real wages, compared to changes in the number of infanticide cases for the first decades of the century, gave a covariance of 82.9 percent (multiple R^2 = .829). Coal prices and real wages supplied the bulk of this correlation, and, as the prices rose, so did the numbers of infanticides (respective slopes = +3.99 and +.671, significant at the 75 percent level). Economic factors explained almost 83 percent of the variation in infanticide cases in accord with the hypothesis proposed at the opening of the chapter. Later in the century, the explanatory power of the combined economic indices had dropped to 32.3 percent (R^2 = .322, significant at the 75 percent level). Coal and wheat prices showed a very low correlation with infanticide. With the coming of the industrial revolution, the price of coal may have begun to reflect the needs of industry rather than the ordinary consumer, and wheat prices were always subject to manipulation. A more sweeping conclusion may be proposed. Behind these figures one discerns, in the beginning of the century, a strong relationship between material improvement and declining infanticide indictments. Once the former had reached a certain level, a floor as it were, their marginal effect—the impact of further increases—upon infanticide began to decline. Material improvements simply did not reach down to any more of the potential offenders, as was suggested earlier in the chapter. Nevertheless, the multiple correlation for both of these periods is high enough to suggest that economic prices and income levels, and the changing quality of life they represented, influenced the commission of infanticide.[22]

The relationship between infanticide and the economic and demographic growth of the New England colonies is more complex. Recent studies of the increasing concentration of wealth in the colonies, the growing scarcity of land, and the increasing population pressure in the oldest New England settlements on the eve of the Revolution, coupled with widely disparate female mortality rates in certain towns early in the century, make simple comparisons with England difficult. In Salem, mortality of females of ages 21 to 30 increased from 21.4 to 37.0 per thousand, from the seventeenth through the eighteenth centuries. In Andover, Massachusetts, the mortality rate for women 20 to 29 years of age increased from 39 to 43.1 per thousand between 1700 and 1759. In Ipswich, in contrast, mortality among females in this age group declined as the century wore on, from 46.3 to 36.8 per thousand. Boston mortality rates varied little during the century.[23]

Broader demographic changes did signal long-term improvement in the quality of childrearing and do correspond to the decline in infanticide indictments. By the end of the eighteenth century, infant mortality rates in most towns had fallen below the lows of the later seventeenth century. Perhaps more important, freer choice in starting families and having children was becoming the rule among young couples. In the growth of premarital pregnancy, younger age at marriage, increasing independence of older children from their parents, and the gradual refusal of parents to give a newborn child the same name as a recently deceased sibling, historians have found signs of modern family structure and sensibility. Whether this meant an increase in affection for children and greater care in childrearing is still a matter of controversy. Historians of childhood in America believe the eighteenth century was an era of ambivalence toward children, ending in improvements in child rearing, if not in more affection. At the very least, the practice of putting out children in the New England colonies was very gradually giving way to the modern nuclear system of child rearing. One would expect infanticide to decline under these conditions and it did.[24]

While the connection between medical and economic improvement, on the one hand, and the decline in infanticide, on the other, is strong enough to substantiate the quality of life thesis, the connection is hardly definitive. (Path analysis of the eighteenth-century environmental causes of infanticide appears in Appendix 3.) In the same manner that economic hardship influenced infanticide through the filter of culture and stress-handling mechanisms in the early seventeenth-century, so material improvement affected infanticide through the filter of social impulses and customs. Changing economic and medical conditions directed their influence upon the rates of infanticide through the medium of the personal feelings and expectations of mothers for their children, and society for its mothers' conduct. These, as we have seen, changed as the eighteenth century wore on, redirecting the impact of environmental forces upon the lives and conduct of parents.

The calculations in this chapter confirm a number of hypotheses about the relative impact upon numbers of indictments, on the one hand, of selective prosecution by authorities and, on the other hand, of environmental factors. First, environmental causal factors are not strong enough to displace completely the attitudes of lawmakers and magistrates as determinants of the volume of indictments. The full explanation must be more complex, for, as the reader has seen, the attitudes of judicial authorities were themselves grounded upon social and economic realities. In the late sixteenth and early seventeenth centuries, social and economic disorder induced justices, already sensitized by religious ideals, to ferret out and severely punish infanticide suspects. In the eighteenth century, material improvement, coupled with new social values, helped to lead judges and juries to revise their views of the crime and the defendant. To be sure, the attitudes of justices did not cause the crime. And some defendants were guilty as charged of murder. Upon these latter, environmental forces had both direct and indirect effects.

6

Individual Motivation

Human motives pulse behind every criminal statistic. This concluding chapter speculates about why people in the early modern Anglo-American world may have committed the crime of infanticide. Historical analysis rests upon implicit concepts of human motive: in the present case, the motives of officials, juries, neighbors and entire communities as well as suspects. Simple behavioral reductions of motivation will not serve; it is not enough to say that the vast majority of murdering mothers did away with their newborn bastards to avoid the shame and difficulty of rearing unwanted illegitimate children. Such reasoning, while a fair summary of the statistics, does not explain why 95 percent of the unmarried women who brought bastards into the world did not murder the children. Nor does it explain the murder of older, legitimate children by their parents and caretakers.

The search for individual motivation in infanticide cases is complicated by the fact that, for most of the period under scrutiny, English and colonial courts were not concerned with questions of motive, but only of fact. The motive of the defendant does not generally appear in records or file papers, until the later *OBSP*'s. The first evidence of infanticidal motives is the plea of temporary insanity, including testimony about amnesia, dissociation, and depression during labor and delivery. Long before the eighteenth century, courts asked pardons for idiots incompetent from birth and lunatics of long-standing who had been convicted of capital crimes. Madness, not a medical term but a legal one, did not "excuse" a homicide, but averted the death penalty. The patent rolls record numerous pardons in infanticide cases: in the period from 1558 to 1575, there were 13 pardons for spinsters convicted of murdering their newborns immediately upon delivery. Without a pardon, however, lunatics might be left in prison until conditions there settled their fate. In Essex, Dorcas Tyndall was recorded a lunatic for the murder of her eight-year-old child and died in prison. If no one would step forward to take care of such a person, she remained in custody of the crown.[1]

Temporary insanity was neither a defense nor a road to pardon in the seventeenth century, but in the next 100 years it gradually became a successful plea to a charge of infanticide. Chief Justice Matthew Hale reported what appears to be an infanticide excused for temporary mental incapacity:

> In the year 1668 at Aylesbury a married woman of good reputation having delivered of a child and not having slept many nights fell into a temporary phrenzy and kild her infant in the absence of any company; but company coming in, she told them that she had killed her infant, and there it lay; she was brought to gaol presently, and after some sleep she recovered her understanding, but marvelled how or why she came thither; she was indicted for murder, and upon her trial the whole matter appearing it was left to the jury with this direction, that if it did appear, that she had any use of reason when she did it, they were to find her guilty; but if they found her under a phrenzy, tho by reason of her late delivery and want of sleep, they should acquit her; that had there been an occasion to move her to this fact, as to hide her shame, which is ordinarily the case of such as are delivered of bastard children and destroy them; or if there had been

jealousy in her husband, that the child had been none of his, or if she hid the infant, or denied the fact, these had been evidences, that the phrenzy was counterfeit; but none of these appearing, and the honesty and virtuous deportment of the woman in her health being known to the jury, and many circumstance of insanity appearing, the jury found her not guilty to the satisfaction of all that heard it.

The defendant's marital state gave credence to her claim of temporary madness. In the eighteenth century, unmarried defendants were able to use similar defenses.[2]

Seen through the lens of modern psychopathology, psychogenic infanticidal motivation appears even more clearly. Psychological classifications distinguish two types of infanticides—both of which can be found in the early modern legal records. These are neonaticide by an unmarried woman and murder of legitimate older children by a mother, and less often, a father. In neonaticide, parental murder of infants within 24 hours of their birth, the murderers are overwhelmingly female, and can be divided into two subcategories. Extremely passive mothers, facing illegitimate birth, may feel shame and guilt which destruction of the infant relieves. This is often accompanied by passive ego defenses like denial of the pregnancy and dissociative reaction (that is, losing track of what was done with the child and by whom). These responses are genuine. A suspect like Anne Haywood may have been telling the truth to the Middlesex jury when she vowed that she did not remember being pregnant. Neonaticide of this type is a form of stress disorder, which mothers with "weak personality structures" undergo. A father may kill an infant for similar reasons, but cases of this type are extremely rare. Neonaticides are also performed by mothers with very strong "instinctual drives" and few "ethical restraints." These offenders tend to be older, more promiscuous women who may repeat the crime. Murdering mothers of this type have a character disorder which at its extreme borders upon psychopathological hostility and impulsiveness. In 1584, Alice Adcock, who was living with an innkeeper, clubbed a constable. She refused to come to court to explain or answer for this and other complaints. In 1589, she was tried and convicted for the murder of her newborn bastard. Cases like hers may be examples of the second neonatal category.[3]

It is not so easy to uncover psychological evidence of the passive form of psychogenic neonaticide. Nevertheless, in two eighteenth-century cases tried in London the legal record does show evidence of denial and dissociation. A butcher's unmarried maidservant, Jane Cooper, carried her strangled infant around for two days, wrapped in rags. Cooper was convicted and executed. Frances Robinson confessed to the five-week-old murder of her newborn infant. She pleaded that she had been "ill" at the time of delivery and dropped the newborn into a privy vault. Her admission of temporary derangement and her contrition moved the jury of acquit her of all charges. Twentieth-century legal and medical authorities would later classify these acts under the rubrics "exhaustive psychosis" and "post partum depression," but almost two centuries passed before statutes eased the penalties for such crimes.[4]

"Filicide," parental murder of a child older than one day, may have a number of origins. The child may aggrevate latent psychotic states in parents by becoming a rival for affection of a spouse (the "Media complex"), or by becoming one parent's weapon against an absent mate. Sometimes the eventual child murderer of this type has a history of aggressive behavior toward the child. On July 3, 1589, a coroner's inquest in the county of Essex examined the body of Joan Knight. She was the eight-year-old daughter of a fisherman and was beaten to death over a period of time by her stepmother, Agnes. Perhaps her stepmother thought Joan was unruly, and the beatings constituted an "accidental" cause of death. A stepmother's revenge against a daughter-rival erupting into violent psychotic range is not unknown. Parents and stepparents' rage toward unwanted children appears in popular literature and psychiatric reports as well as criminal records.[5]

By far the most numerous variety of filicides in the mod-

ern records are "altruistic suicides." Phillip Resnick has concluded that altruistic suicide accounts for over half the murders of children over one day in age. Child murderers of
this type, mainly women because they spend more time
rearing children than men, may conclude that they cannot
abandon their children when they commit suicide, or de-
lude themselves that the child is suffering so much that it
has to be killed, or believe themselves and their children
persecuted. In cases of this type, the child may be a contributor to the suicidal intent of its eventual murderer by cre-
ating domestic pressures which a latently psychotic parent
cannot handle. After the murder of the child, the parent
sometimes feels a great release of tension. It is not uncom-
mon in these cases for the parent to experience temporary
amnesia, or to hallucinate that someone had forced them to
kill the child.[6] On the fifth of October, 1584, Martha Godfrey tried to convince a Middlesex jury that the devil had
made her use a butcher knife on her child. She would not
plead guilty or confess her own part, and the sincerity of
her delusions put punishment off for a time at least. Dorothy Talbie's murder of their daughter was probably an altruistic suicide that stopped short of self-murder. In 1705,
Essex husbandman John Heyden cut his eight-year-old
daughter Anne's throat with a knife, then killed himself.
His death was ruled a suicide, hers a murder. Mary Hindes
was a widow who told a Middlesex jury that she would
"rather die than live" when tried for drowning an 18-
month-old child left in her care. Witnesses testified she had
fits of insanity in which she threatened to commit suicide,
but had been very fond of the child before she murdered
it. In 1732, "Richard Smith and his wife killed their infant
daughter, hanged themselves, and left a long letter com-
plaining that life was not worth living."[7]

There is a fine line between psychological breakdown and
inflamed susceptibility to superstition. In conduct today
termed "maladjusted," or paranoid and delusional, but
which occurred among both married and unmarried men
and women in early modern societies, fear of the devil led

to infanticide. Before baptism, the infant lay outside the protection of the church. A malformed child might be a "changeling," already in the devil's power. Fears of witches' spells mingled in these cases with folk superstitions, the results of which could be a sudden fatal "accident" to the child, followed by a hurried burial. Less superstitious, but equally dangerous to the infant, was the parent's attempt to beat the devil out of him. Correction of children and servants, amounting to regular corporal punishment, was not prohibited in English or colonial law or custom. The rod was not spared, and one popular manual enjoined:

> If thy child be rebel and will not bow them low,
> If any of them misdo neither curse not blow;
> But take a smart rod and beat them in a row
> Till they cry mercy and their guilt well know.

The same advice could be found in the New World. In Plymouth, one master was found guilty of manslaughter for bruising, lashing, freezing, and otherwise abusing his servant up to the moment of the latter's death. That the beating went so far without the intervention of authorities in that tiny settlement is evidence of the right to correct which the master and parents possessed.[8]

In an atmosphere of commonplace violence against children of all ages, the killing of some older infants may have begun as seventeenth- and eighteenth-century cases of "child battering." While neglect and indifference have their fatal effects very early in infancy, child battering erupts within families which have given the child some care and love. Brandt F. Steele and Carl Pollack describe the syndrome in terms of "role reversal." When the child does not appear to appreciate the mothering or fathering it receives or does not perform to its parent's expectations, the parent(s) respond as though their own parents were condemning them. Battering parents were generally over-disciplined and under-loved by their own parents, indeed very often battered, and relive in the baby's apparent rejection of their care their own rejection as children. This description of parenting may be more appropriate for the period 1558 to 1803, than for the 1900s. Varying conditions of family economic resources, cohesiveness, and overcrowding also provide stress factors which may make child battery more common. David Gil has argued that child battery is correlated with lower socioeconomic status, and other sociological observers have found that baby battering overlaps other forms of criminal behavior. A last correlate that seems irrefutable is that more babies are battered when the family is broken, the child is illegitimate, or the caretakers are merely living together, than in cohesive nuclear families. These are the same socioeconomic and domestic conditions that one finds in many early modern infanticide cases.[9]

Another argument for the similarity between the modern baby battering case and some infanticides in early modern England and New England lies in the persistence of a "darker side" of motherhood. Psychiatrist J. C. Rheingold has speculated that material violence to children may be a form of "acting out" of violent feeling by some women toward their own mothers. Other clinicians have postulated that in the act of giving birth and first nurture to children, there is a "surging up" of childhood memories in the mother. When these are associated with pain and suppressed aggressive urges in some mothers, they may be turned back upon the child with fatal results:

> Let us again look at the mother in anxiety in the post-partum period. She is beset by conflict, deeper and more desperate than any conflict a man ever experiences. Motherhood is the culmination of her strivings since childhood with satisfaction reaching into her biologic being; it means safe deliverance from the perils of pregnancy and childbirth: it is demonstration of her adequacy as a woman and it allays her haunting fears of female inferiority; it is triumph over all the forces that have sought to defeat her; it is an active achievement; it is revered status in our culture, and it confers fatherhood upon her husband and creates a family. She wishes to love the child and be a good mother. But panic overrides all of these values and gratifications. She feels herself to be in

mortal danger. She has somehow grown up, attained a degree of feminity, married, entered into sexual life, and survived a pregnancy and delivery . . . But having a child is the most forbidden act of self-realization, the ultimate and least pardonable offense.

These forces would have worked with redoubled effect upon the minds of some early modern mothers. From the time that they were children to the stage of their lives when they bore and reared children themselves, they had learned how hard it was to be female. The lot of an average child in that era, compared to our own, was harsh, and female offspring were a greater fiscal burden to their parent than male children. The maturing young woman of early modern England and New England would have perceived the fact that she occupied a lower station in society, at least by official yardsticks, than men born in her family. Finally, the experience of childbirth, a quintessential female act, with its unique dangers and special duties, would remind her of all she had learned about the place of women. The stepmother, the mother of a bastard, the very poor mother, and the deserted or widowed mother, may have experienced all these psychological pressures more acutely in that age than in our own.[10]

The sociological, economic, and psychological parameters of fatal child battering fit cases in early modern court records. The farther one goes back into early modern English and American history, the stronger is the parallel between the domestic circumstances surrounding the murder of some older children and the battering syndrome. The overt intent of child battering parents is not to murder the child, but behind the aggression, if only for a moment, throbs the desire to kill. In some early modern cases, this occurred. In the records of Essex and Middlesex, for the years 1558 through 1624, one of every five cases of suspicious infant death bears some marks of battering. In March 1613, Joan Archer, a widow, was brought before the assize court for fatally wounding her son John with tongs. Anne Inghram, wife of Edward, struck her seven-year-old son Edward Jr.

on the head and later beat him with a whip. He died, but the record does not show his mother's fate. In these Essex cases, the victims exhibited multiple visible signs of violence. Bludgeons, knives, and even blows from the hand, all weapons of an angry parent, were the most frequent causes of death. Each of the victims' families showed some degree of instability—the father was away, the child was an orphan or illegitimate, or a stepmother or lover-accomplice was involved in the suspected crime.[11]

A group of early modern child murders resulting from severe oven burns, a common form of abuse, invites explicit comparison to modern cases. On March 8, 1588, Margaret Yonge burned her seven-year-old son, James, to death in an oven. In remorse, she confessed. Maud Smyth periodically forced her six-year-old son Tom into a hot oven for two and a half weeks, from February 10 until February 17, 1560, until he suffocated. James Yonge was illegitimate; Tom Smyth was not. Maud Smith received the pardon of the crown, because her act seemed mad, while the contrite mother of the illegitimate child went to the gallows. On December 12, 1614, Ann Capell, taking care of two-year-old Abigail Scouler for her parents, "put her so near a fire, willfully and of malice aforethought, that her back, buttocks and thighs were burnt, so that as a result of the said burning on them, she died." Capell was acquitted. These cases strongly resemble a modern episode of child burning reported by journalist Jean Renvoize. It was

> a bizarre and quite horrifying method of punishment. A father found a cruel and drastic way of punishing his three-year-old son for crying. He grabbed hold of the boy and put him in a hot oven. The boy, Anthony H—, screamed with pain, and was pulled out of the oven by his mother. But, by then, he had been badly burned. Words printed on the bottom of the oven were imprinted on his skin.[12]

Many more child battery infanticides undoubtedly escaped detection than came to trial. Only one out of three cases which were reported resulted in conviction, as defendants convinced the courts that death was the result of an accident. Open ovens certainly made such accidents possible. Without modern hospitals, victims of these "accidents" could not be saved—much less proved to be examples of child battering. The accused could also claim that they were merely disciplining an unruly child.[13]

Cases of neurotic neonaticide and child battering to one side, it cannot be said that every case of infanticide or even a majority involved psychosis or character disorders of a diagnosable kind. Nigel Walker has termed some of the neonaticides "rational," for a woman forced to bear the shame of rearing an illegitimate child might well find the situation intolerable. The refusal of defendants like Ann Morris to plead to her indictment at the Middlesex quarter sessions shows that defiance could be as near the surface as submission. "She would not tell a lie for all the world," she said, as she finally admitted the neonaticide. In a recent essay, Robert Malcolmson has given his verdict on these defendants.

> As for the character of these women who killed their babies, although our considerations are almost entirely speculative, it may be suggested that the more vulnerable women were those who had been particularly respectable, well behaved and reputedly virtuous, . . . Women with doubtful reputations, in unsettled circumstances or in casual employments may have envisaged a bastard birth with rather less horror, and consequently have been less motivated to consider concealment at all. . . .[14]

Neonaticide was for some of these vulnerable unwed mothers a deliberate form of delayed abortion. The similarity and relationship between the two crimes is impressive. Both infanticide and abortion were concealed crimes, primarily committed by young, unmarried women who faced an unwanted pregnancy. For poor, unwed mothers who faced the brunt of bastardy prosecutions, concealment of the corpse of a bastard infant would at least prohibit coroners from discovering the cause of death, and at best hide from the magistrates proof that a pregnancy had occurred at all. Before the last half of the nineteenth century, abortion with drugs or instruments was dangerous. For some women it might have appeared safer to have the child, after concealing the pregnancy, and then to perform a delayed abortion. Some, like Amy Munn of Connecticut, might have attempted abortion before attempting infanticide. An unwed mother might have waited, in vain, for the father of her infant to marry her, until it was too late for an abortion. Despite the latent injunction of the Jacobean infanticide statute against abortion, evidence from one witness of death before the infant's independent existence was sufficient to establish innocence of the charge. If the child was killed before it was fully removed from the vaginal cavity, according to Hale, "it was no felony," for the child was not *"in rerum natura."* [15]

There were cases which civil authorities investigated for evidence of infanticide that seem to be delayed abortions. In 1611, Margaret Lyveston, a widow, and three men were charged at the Middlesex quarter sessions court "for delivering one Jane Peckeham of a child, in the fields, which said child being dead is suspected to have been wronged by the said Margaret, being a midwife . . ." The fact that the entire affair took place in the fields, a secluded spot to which the company had removed themselves, suggests to the scholar, as it might have suggested to the justices, that Lyveston was performing a delayed abortion. Five years later, John Robinson, a baker, and three other men were called before the magistrates in London "to answer concerning the death of a young infant born of the body of Dorothy Mowbrow, who was removed on a chair out of their parish of St. Andres, Holborn, into the parish of St. Giles in the Fields, whereby it is supposed that the child miscarried and received a hurt in the head, whereof it died. . . ." The object of this procession may have been to avoid the penalties of the bastardy laws or to perform a secret infanticide. A coroner's inquest concluded that the child was born alive and died later from exposure. Concealment was the common feature of these delayed abortions, and magistrates invariably investigated them.[16]

The assistance of friends, lovers, midwives, neighbors, and others in the suspicious death and concealment of bastards smacks of abortion "rings," save only that the infant was to be destroyed after birth. Joan Penekemes kept a house in London to which an unmarried woman in labor might retire to bear her child and return to the world without it. Ann Stratton went there in the fall of 1609 and gave birth to a male child. The quarter sessions court, under its commissions of oyer and terminer and general gaol delivery, found her guilty of the murder of the child. Rachel White, another resident of this house, was cleared of murdering her female infant; a coroner's jury declared it stillborn. The midwife, Elizabeth Rawlings, the wife of Edward Rawlings, Penekemes, and her other female associates, were gaoled for "bringing lewd women abed in suspecting places" and for concealing the deaths of bastard infants. Over the next five years, the London magistrates closed down three other establishments for "harboring lewd persons" and transporting or concealing illegitimate newborns.[17]

The oaths administered in England and Massachusetts to midwives by church authorities were directed against both abortion and infanticide:

> I, [name], admitted to the office and occupation of a midwife, will faithfully and diligently exercise the said office according to such cunning and knowledge as God hath given me: . . . I will not permit or suffer that woman being in labour or travail shall name any other to be the father of her child, than only he who is the right and true father thereof; and that I will not suffer any other body's child to be set, brought or laid before any woman delivered of child in the place of her natural child, so far forth as I can know and understand. Also, I will not use any kind of sorcery or incantation in the time of the travail of any woman; and that I will not destroy the child born of any woman, nor cut, nor pull off the head

thereof, or otherwise dismember or hurt the same, or suffer it to be so hurt or dismembered, by any manner of ways or means . . . .

The clergymen who officiated at these oaths knew that canon law classed abortion with infanticide.[18]

Justices and clerics in London and Boston may have been suspicious of these cases for another reason. The participants may have belonged to that class of urban residents who had little regard for law or magistrates. Antisocial tendencies may be intensified by an urban environment, especially one marked with overcrowding, relative economic deprivation, and continuous conflict. Howard Jones, an English criminologist, has recognized such conditions in the "tough neighborhoods" of modern English cities. Earlier English and American observers perceived the same dangers in seventeenth- and eighteenth-century cities. Within such environments, the "norms" of the denizens permit a much higher level of aggression than was tolerated in the larger culture. Childhood in these subcultures was and is cruel, and an individual child may have little intrinsic worth to his or her adult caretakers. In this subculture of deprivation, violence, and crime, exploitation of children verged on the normal. Unscrupulous or corrupt women, like the besotted mother in the foreground of Hogarth's drawing of "Gin Lane," were assumed capable of the disposal of their unwanted progeny. If an infant was murdered by its parent or caretaker in this setting, it is unlikely that neighbors would report the crime.[19]

Motivation for the crime of infanticide was as varied as the personalities of the men and women who attempted it and the situations in which they found themselves. External pressures like social ostracism, shame, loss of employment and reputation, and forcible intercourse, were certainly motives for the crimes, but before any individual would undertake it, these influences had to pass through the filter of individual character and perception. Outside forces created stress, but response to stress was not uniform. When fear and anger were overwhelming enough to cause the perpetrator to view the child as a thing, a cancer or a foreign object, or to make the perpetrator believe that such injustices as led to the conception and would follow from successful birth were unsupportable, the crime might follow. The assistance rendered by neighbors, lovers, parents, and paid agents may mean that such reasoning was acceptable in certain quarters. Between the disoriented and the "rational" infanticidal parents and caretakers, lay men and women, parents of newborns or slightly older children, frustrated at their own lives and unable to reach back into their own childhoods for resources to nurture the growth of the new lives entrusted to them, who struck out at the immediate cause of their misery. The newborn after a difficult birth, the crying infant, and the disobedient toddler became the victims.

Epilogue

The Continuing Crime

The repeal of 21 James I c. 27 closed an era in the development of jurists' and jurors' attitudes toward the crime of infanticide. Growing leniency in the courts and declining rates of indictment were connected not merely by the indifference of informants to the offense or officials' unwillingness to prosecute, but by more enduring bonds of changing domestic customs and sentiment. Our story ends here, but infanticide does not. Improvements in the standard of living among the poor, greater affection within the domestic circle, and the increasing importance of children in Anglo-American society may have reduced the incidence of the crime, and official mercy mitigated punishment for it, but infanticide survived.

In the mid-nineteenth century, controversy about infanticide again appeared in England. Middlesex county coroner Edwin Lankster reported to medical audiences that 22 percent of his inquests were upon the bodies of murdered children. By the 1860s 150 dead infants were found each year upon the streets and in the waters of the metropolis. William Burke Ryan, a fellow of the Royal College of Surgeons and a well-known medical writer, cited case after case of infants found floating in the Thames or strangled and left bundled in alleys—a total of 298 coroners' verdicts of willful murder for the years 1855 to 1860. The horrors were not over. During the winter of 1895 and 1896, 40 bodies of newborns were found in the Thames. The infants had been strangled. These and other infant murders were traced to a Mrs. Dyer and her son, Arthur Palmer, who ran a "baby farm" at Caversham, Reading. For a fee, they disposed of unwanted infants, first killing the child, then concealing its corpse. Dyer was executed in 1896, but a gruesome rhyme commemorating her crime remained popular: "The old baby farmer has been executed;/It's quite time she was put out of the way./She was a bad woman, it is not disputed;/Not a word in her favor can anyone say." [1]

During the same years, American state courts regularly tried mothers for infanticide. In antebellum South Carolina, at least five women were indicted, and one was hanged, for the murder of newborns. Virginia slaves were widely suspected of overlaying their children, although some of these deaths may have been caused by "crib death." In New York City, Lydia Sherman poisoned her own family, including two children, then moved to Corum, Connecticut, poisoned a new husband, and ended her career by marrying and murdering a widower and her new stepchildren. Cases of infanticide occurred across the country. A standard American treatise on criminal law at the turn of this century cited infanticide precedents from California, Pennsylvania, and South Carolina to show that mere concealment did not prove guilt of murder. Other cases from Texas and New York were used to illustrate the English doctrine of *in rerum natura*. [2]

Reports of the crime remain front page news. On Sunday, July 28, 1978, the *Miami Herald* reported the terror of Fraline Harris, 16, as she watched the two-month-old daughter she had beaten to death lowered into the earth. In Columbus, Ohio, two weeks of headline newspaper coverage followed the indictment of Margo Davies for the multiple murder of her three infants. The body of a newborn infant was found under a bed at a well-known girls' school in Farmington, Connecticut. Medical examiners believed the child died about two hours after its birth. In Chicago, a woman was tried and convicted for dumping her one-month-old daughter into an incinerator. Despite the absence of the corpse, the confession of the 17-year-old-mother led to her incarceration. Some of these crimes are neonaticides, others are fatal child batterings. The defendants' motives are familiar: feelings of depression, anger, shame and rejection as powerful as those felt by previous generations of infanticidal parents.[3]

The overall modern figures for infant murder are small in one sense—rarely more than 3 percent of all United States murder victims in the 1960s—but they still loom large in public consciousness. In the United States, an average of slightly over 100 infants up to a year old were killed each year from 1961 to 1974. About 3.4 percent of all murders were parental infanticides. The figures for England and Wales in the same period are slightly larger, but the number of murders there is but 3 percent of the total in the United States. In England and Wales, an average of six trials for infanticide occur each year, out of over 150 trials for murder. These figures are somewhat deceiving, for in both the United States and England and Wales violent crimes rose ahead of population increases in the 1960s and the 1970s. In the United States, 3008 murders were reported to the FBI in 1961, of which 59 had victims under one year of age. In 1976, there were 16,605 murders, with 182 victims under one year. The percentage of murders that are infanticides has dipped from the eighteenth century to the present, and the per capital figures of indictments (not to mention actual crime rates) has surely fallen, but the crime persists.[4]

The changes in official response to the crime which commenced during the eighteenth century have continued into the present. In England, over the period between 1905 and 1921, 60 women were convicted of infanticide, but sentences for 59 of them were commuted. In 1922, a new "felony of infanticide" reduced fatal assault upon one's own "newly born" child to a manslaughter. The term "newly born" in the 1922 statute was defined in 1938 to mean "within the first year of life." The murder of an older child retained its definition as a murder under the 1929 Infant Life Preservation Act, with a penalty of up to life imprisonment. Concealment of bastardy remained a crime as well during this period. State criminal statutes in the United States vary, but juries and judges have leaned to the side of mercy. Women convicted of murdering newborns are often released after mental observation, with provision for continuing outpatient psychiatric care. Long prison sentences are not common, but may be growing in frequency very recently. Death is no longer meted out, although it remains on the books in many states, including those in New England.[5]

In the light of what is known today about the crime of infanticide, the rise of modern infanticide law may be reviewed. In the period between 1558 and 1803, infanticide became a highly visible offense in England and New England courts. Though infanticide was never a very common crime, lawmakers and judges developed a sensitivity to bastardy and immorality among the poor, resulting in noteworthy increases in indictments for infanticide. Those prosecuted for the murder of infants were overwhelmingly mothers who violated the statutes against sexual continence or domestic order—unmarried women guilty of fornication or married women known to use violence against their children. Economic distress and social disorder drove women to the crime in increasing numbers. In both England and New England, the first response of authorities to their own discovery of infanticide was harsh law, unyieldingly enforced. These steps led to raised percentages of conviction. A century later, in slow but inexorable fashion, changing community standards on sexual conduct and revised views of the character of mothers undermined the moral basis of the campaign against infanticide. Better living standards reduced the number of infanticides. Where murder could be proven, infanticide was severely punished, but suspects were again given the benefit of the doubt. The end of the eighteenth century saw the reversal of the trends in prosecutions and convictions that had marked the beginning of the seventeenth century, and the relaxation of severe statutes on the crime.

Throughout this process, England and New England followed parallel courses. Allowing for differences in absolute numbers, the rise and fall of indictment and conviction for the crime in the two jurisdictions traced the same curve. The differences in environment were not important factors. By the end of the eighteenth century, legal and social changes in England and New England had wrought the same revolution in treatment of the suspected infanticidal parent. In neither place did reform erase infanticide. Instead, the crime was reduced to a low but steady rate of commission. To understand what lay behind this hard core of infanticides, we attempted to reconstruct the motives of individual defendants. These persisted in the face of legal and social improvements. They ranged from "rational" responses to sexual violation and portending ostracism, to severe psychotic episodes, a depth and variety of feeling found in cases today.

Reform of law and punishment cannot eradicate a crime whose motives lie deep within social stresses and family conflicts. Ostracism for a child out of wedlock or indifference to a child of poverty are pressures upon the mother soon displaced upon the child. The child, the cause of social displeasure, becomes its immediate victim. The appearance of 15-to-18-year-old women, poor unwed mothers of infants, among defendants today recalls the suspects and motives of our earlier period of study. One can only conclude that if local authorities and kinship networks give support to the unwed or overburdened mother, the likelihood of her frustration and anger mortally falling upon the child or the child-to-be are greatly reduced. Childrearing practices have an influence on potential infant murders at generations' distance. If the childhood of new parents was a warm and trusting experience, they are more likely to regard having their own children as a positive and worthwhile enterprise. Only then will infanticide disappear.

Appendix 1

Multiple Classification Analysis of Verdicts from Tudor-Stuart England and Colonial Massachusetts

The verdict jurors rendered against suspects for infanticide was motivated by the circumstances and status of the defendant and her victim, as well as by evidence of the crime. Among the most important of the former considerations before the jurors were the legitimacy and the age of the victim and the marital status of the defendant. This book offers measures of association between each of these independent variables and the verdict of the court. No matter how elaborate cross-tabulations may be, they cannot take into account the simultaneous effects of the other independent variables upon the events under study. Facts like the illegitimacy of the newborn child and the unmarried state of the mother had a compound effect upon the jurors' deliberations. Technically speaking, one must "adjust" the relationship between each of the independent variables and the verdict for the effects of the other independent variables, to learn what effect each independent variable would have upon the jurors' decision if, in all other respects, the defendants and their victims were exactly alike. Multiple Classification Analysis (MCA), a statistical output of the "analysis of variance" subprogram of SPSS, permits examination of the effects of up to five categorical variables like legitimacy and marital status upon the verdict, while controlling for the effects of the other four.[1]

MCA requires an interval level dependent variable, but "verdict" is only a category. One may sidestep this difficulty by treating a not guilty verdict as a "o," and a guilty verdict as a "1." This turns the verdict into a "dummy" interval variable. Table A1.1 below traces the effects of three categorical independent variables upon the verdicts of Tudor and early Stuart infanticide juries. The tests for statistical significance for these effects were less than satisfactory, no better than the 75 percent level, but the MCA is still informative. The "grand mean" in the second column is .56, which means that 56 percent of the verdicts were guilty (the dummy value of 1). The N is the number of cases in each of the categories of the three independent variables. The "unadjusted deviation" in column four is the number of percentage points the particular independent variable is above or below the mean—its effect upon the verdict—without holding the other independent variables constant. The smaller the N of cases, the less reliable these deviations are. Eta is the strength of each independent variable's relationship with the verdict of the jurors, before adjustment for the effects of the other variables. The next column gives deviation from the mean after adjustment—again, the effect the fact had on the jury—controlling for the other independent variables' effects. The beta in column seven is the equivalent of the partial correlation coefficient: the strength of the relationship between the verdict and the independent variable, removing the interference of the other independent variables.[2]

Of the independent variables shown above, only legitimacy changes its effect and power of association very much

[1] Jae-On Kim and Frank J. Kohout, "Analysis of Variance and Covariance" in Norman H. Nie, et al., *Statistical Package for the Social Sciences* (2d ed, New York, 1975), 400–422.

[2] Richard Jensen, "New Presses for Old Grapes: I: Multiple Classification Analysis," *Historical Methods* 11 (Fall, 1978), 174.

Table A1.1
Multiple Classification Analysis
of Infanticide Cases in England,
Essex, Hertfordshire, Middlesex and Sussex, 1558–1648[a]

Verdict by Legitimacy of the Victim
Age of the Victim
Marital Status of the Accused

Variables	N	Unadjusted		Adjusted for Independents	
		Deviation	Eta	Deviation	Beta
Legitimacy of Victim					
1 Yes	20	−0.01		−0.14	
2 No	115	0.00		0.02	
			0.01		0.12
Age of Victim					
1 Neonate	118	−0.01		−0.02	
2 Under Two	12	0.02		0.08	
3 Under Nine	5	0.24		0.36	
			0.10		0.15
Marital Status of Defendant					
1 Married	25	−0.00		0.02	
2 Single	105	0.01		0.00	
3 Widowed	5	−0.16		−0.16	
			0.07		0.07

Multiple R Squared = .020
Multiple R   = .140
186 Cases were processed
Fifty-one Cases were missing (27.4 percent).

[a]*Grand Mean* = 0.56 (56 percent conviction rate).

after adjustment. When legitimate children were victims, their cases ended in convictions 55 percent of the time (0.01 deviation from the grand mean), but when we adjust for the effect of the age of victim and the marital status of the accused on the minds of jurors, the conviction rate for cases involving legitimate victims drops to 42 percent (0.14 percentage point deviation from the grand mean). In effect, had the jury not known about the marital status of the accused or age of the victim they would have weighed the legitimacy of the victim far more heavily in favor of the defendant than they did. Beta = .12 is still small, but it is larger than eta (= .01) and thus runs in the correct direction to support the conclusion above. The other independent variables do not show any noteworthy changes.

The intertwining of circumstances like the legitimacy of the victims and the marital status of the defendants in jurors' perceptions is also apparent in Massachusetts, in Table A1.2. The change that adjustment made in the deviation of categories of "legitimacy" from the grand mean, here .34, is very similar to that in MCA Table A1.1. When the relationship between verdict and legitimacy is measured with victim age and defendants' marital status held constant, the relationship grows stronger, in the logical direction. Before adjustment, the question of legitimacy made little difference to jurors apart from the closely allied issues of the victim's age and the marital status of the defendant. When the effects of the latter were controlled, the legitimacy of the victim contributed to a 23 percentage point lower than average conviction rate. The establishment of the illegitimacy of the child resulted in a conviction rate 5 percentage points higher than the average. The adjusted figures involved swings of 24 and 4 percentage points respectively. As one would expect, the strength of correlation also increases, from an eta = .04 to beta = .26. These are not really different (they are both essentially zero), but the changes are suggestive. The overall change in the influence of victim's age upon verdict was not large, and the categories with the largest alteration of percentages—"under two" and "under nine" years of age—were those with very small numbers of cases. The effect of marital status shows a change after adjustment for multiple effects. Proof of marriage affected jurors' decisions in the context of the legitimacy and age of the child. When these latter are held constant (in effect, removed from the sight of the jurors) the married woman accused of murdering her child was 12 percentage points (.16 to .28 deviation) more likely to be convicted than she would have been when juries were apprised of victim age

Table A1.2
Multiple Classification Analysis
of Infanticide Cases in Massachusetts, 1630–1780[a]

Verdict by Legitimacy of the Victim
Age of the Victim
Marital Status of the Accused

Variables	N	Unadjusted		Adjusted for Independents	
		Deviation	Eta	Deviation	Beta
Legitimacy of Victim					
1 Yes	10	−0.04		−0.28	
2 No	51	0.01		0.05	
			0.04		
Age of Victim					0.26
1 Neonate	49	0.00		0.01	
2 Under Two	7	−0.20		−0.29	
3 Under Nine	5	0.26		0.27	
			0.21		0.26
Marital Status of Defendant					
1 Married	20	0.16		0.28	
2 Single	39	−0.06		−0.12	
3 Widowed	2	−0.34		−0.41	
			0.25		0.42
Multiple R Square					0.169
Multiple R					0.411

Seventy-six Cases were processed,
Fifteen Cases were "missing" (did not have data on all three variables. All effects significant at 85 percent level or better).

[a]*Grand mean* = 0.34 (34 percent conviction rate).

and legitimacy. Marriage itself, as in the cross-tabulations
early in Chapter 2, did not save defendants without sup-
porting evidence of legitimacy of victims. Controlling for
marital status actually lowered the risk that single women
faced before infanticide tribunals from a 28 percent conviction rate (a deviation of .06 from the grand mean) to a 22
percent conviction rate (a .12 deviation from the grand mean).
Again, these shifts are not statistically very significant, but
they are worth discussing. Spinsterhood worked against a
suspect when joined to testimony that the child was a new-

born bastard. The low betas for the final adjustments means that the relationship among concealment, illegitimacy, spinsterhood, the youth of victim, and the jury verdict were truly cumulative. It was the way these facts fit together into a pattern of opportunity and motive that led juries to their verdicts.

MCA confirms and expands our understanding of the complex process of judgment of infanticide by jurors. Efforts in this direction are limited by the absence of the reliable data on some variables—particularly the question of concealment—reducing the number of cases one can submit to MCA. The more numerous the crimes and the fuller the information on them, the more significant and broad this manner of statistical presentation will become.

Appendix 2

Correction for Missing Court Records

The assizes met twice a year except during the civil war years of 1643 and 1644. Unfortunately, not all of the records of these sittings have been preserved. Murder, manslaughter, and infanticide cases occurred at almost every session, and more often than not were settled at that session. Undoubtedly a number of cases of fatal violence are overlooked in the pages above because records are lost or destroyed. Would these records, if they had been preserved, change the conclusions in this book? It is possible to ignore the missing records and the cases therein, and compare indictments of types of homicide whose record has survived. It is also possible to take the missing data into account. These sittings took place, and it is as realistic to seek some way to approximate the missing case loads as it is to disregard them. Any formula must avoid both exaggeration and minimization of the missing data. The same formula must be applied to all homicides in the extant assize records. The fewer records that are missing, the more reliable the correction should be. For successive four-year periods, the number of actually recorded indictments was taken, divided by the number of assize sittings in which these cases

Table A2.1
Corrected Aggressive Stress, Essex 1558–1647[a]

Period	Number of Assizes for which Records exist (eight were supposed to meet)	Corrected Infanticide	Corrected Murder and Manslaughter (of adults)
1560–1563	2	3.00	32.0
1564	6	5.33	9.33
1568	5	3.20	12.8
1572	7	1.14	6.86
1576	7	3.40	16.0
1580	7	5.70	28.6
1584	8	4.00	14.0
1588	8	4.00	25.0
1592	8	3.00	22.0
1596	5	3.20	19.2
1600	7	3.40	36.6
1604	1	insufficient data	
1608	8	6.00	22.0
1612	6	2.70	12.0
1616	7	3.43	12.6
1620	3	8.00	13.3
1624	5	9.60	20.8
1628	6	12.00	20.0
1632	6	8.00	10.7
1636	6	5.33	5.33
1640	4	6.00	14.0
1644	5	11.20	11.2

[a]$R^2 = .221, b = .833.$

appeared, and then multiplied by the number of missing sessions. This correction was then added to the number of recorded cases to get an "expected" number of cases. The results of correction of various crimes are geometrically related, and could alter the variances (R^2) in regressions. An example: If in a given four year period one found three recorded cases of infanticide in the records of seven sittings of the Essex assizes (of eight that actually met), the correction would proceed (three cases/seven sittings) times (one missing sitting) plus three cases equals 3.43 "expected" cases.

Correction of murder and infanticide cases of Tudor-Stuart Essex is given in Table A2.1. Regression of corrected infanticide with corrected murder and manslaughter gives an R^2 = .221, larger than the uncorrected R^2 = .149. The "expected" numbers of cases of these crimes slightly raises the correlation coefficient. The slope for the corrected table was b = .833, showing slightly more influence of murderous aggression upon infanticide than the uncorrected slope of b = .371.

The same formula was used to "correct" data for missing records from the quarter sessions of Essex, in order to compare "expected" bastardy with "expected" infanticide. Defendants in bastardy cases appear in more than one session of the quarter sessions court about one time in five, and more than twice about 5 percent of the time. The correction of bastardy was therefore multiplied by a constant of .75, to remove the effect of duplication of cases. The corrected data appear in Table A2.2. In this table, R^2 = .151, b = .848, with results significant at the 75 percent level. Regression of

Table A2.2
Corrected Infanticide and Bastardy, Essex, 1576–1619[a]

Period	*Extant Quarter Sessions (16 were supposed to meet)*	*Corrected Infanticide*[b]	*Corrected Bastardy*
1576–1579	13	3.40	18.8
1580	12	5.70	16.3
1584	14	4.00	17.7
1588	16	4.00	20.0
1592	13	3.00	17.6
1596	14	3.20	25.5
1600	15	3.40	44.1
1604	3	insufficient data	
1608	13	6.00	24.6
1612	15	2.70	37.8
1616	15	3.43	36.8

[a] R^2 = .151, b = .848.
[b] The number of assize sittings extant, and the computation of the corrected infanticide indictments, appears above in Table A2.1.

corrected Essex bastardy and infanticide cases slightly lowered the covariation of the two, and moved the slope closer to that found in Middlesex.

Correction of criminal data to compensate for missing assize and sessions records does not drastically alter interpretations of the relationship among crimes. Correction acts as a check on conclusions based upon incomplete sources, sometimes increasing, sometimes decreasing, the variance. If the variances were higher in the first place, such corrections might be much more important to understanding crimes than it is now.

Appendix 3

~~~~~~~~~~~~~~

Path Analysis of the
Environmental Causes of Infanticide

Path analysis, combining all regression results into a graphic illustration of causal sequences, depends upon adherence to certain basic concepts. In path analysis, one attempts to make explicit the causal assumptions of an historical analysis. It is a tool to test, interpret, and display, but not uncover causes. In this study, path analysis is advanced in only the most tentative way, but the technical requirements of path analysis are met. These may be divided into seven headings: 1, interval scale measurement; 2, low homoscedasticity; 3, low multicollinearity; 4, linear additive relationships between the variables; 5, nonrecursiveness; 6, completeness of the model; and 7, a high degree of measurement reliability and validity.[1]

Path coefficients are identical to the beta weights (the standardized *b* coefficients) in multiple regressions. The path coefficient is the amount of change in the variable at the right or head of the arrow which results from a one unit

[1] Otis L. Duncan, "Path Analysis: Sociological Examples," *American Journal of Sociology* 72 (July, 1966), 1; G. T. Nygreen, "Interactive Path Analysis," *American Sociologist* 6 (February, 1971), 41; Herbert B. Asher, *Causal Modelling* (Beverly Hills, 1976), 29–61.

change in the variable at the left or tail of the arrow. Path models move from independent variables at the left side of the model to the dependent variables at its right side. Error, residual, or exogenous effects on each of the variables are calculated conventionally by $\sqrt{1 - R^2}$, where R^2 is the multiple R^2 of all variables. Path diagram A3.1 follows these rules.[2]

Returning to the seven criteria for diagram A3.1 one finds: first, the variables are all interval level data introduced in Chapter 5. Second, although homoscedasticity has no convenient measure, it is the degree of common variance of the error terms and its avoidance is a major objective of the design. No sequential common variation effect (i.e. due to time) exists, for the Durkin-Waston statistic is 1.97, when 2.00 indicates no effect. Third, the highest collinearity among all the variables was that of .52 between bastardy and witchcraft, well below any danger level. Fourth, no trend in the data bars a linear procedure like regression. Fifth, the left-right positioning of the variables offers a reasonable causal hypothesis. Sixth, as the entire discussion in Chapter 5 bears witness, the variables used were the best indicators of a complete model of infanticide. The odd man out is birth control, but this does not appear to effect any of the variables involved in systematic fashion. It is reasonable to assume these effects are spread randomly over the entire model. Seventh, these measures of criminal activity are as reliable and valid as any for this period. It is this last criterion which renders the path analysis so tentative. The frailty of these sources cannot be overcome by statistical manipulation. Nevertheless, if the path analysis model advances understanding even slightly beyond where we stood with only the criminal record, it was worth the effort.

The model does reveal relationships not otherwise visible. Asocialization evidently does not act directly upon infanticide, but can greatly influence that crime through the two

[2] Jae-on Kim and Frank J. Kohout, "Special Topics in General Linear Models," in Norman H. Nie, et al., *Statistical Package for the Social Sciences* (2d. ed., New York, 1975), 383–392.

Path Diagram A3.1
Tentative Causes of Infanticide
in Middlesex, 1612 - 1618

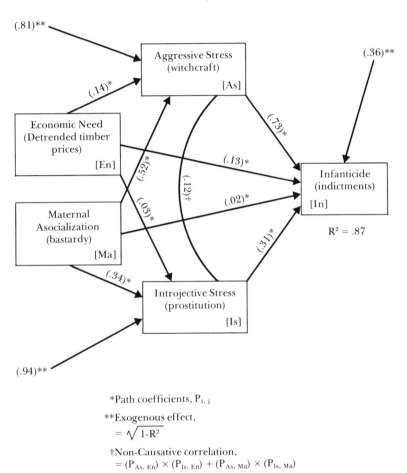

(.81)**

Aggressive Stress
(witchcraft)

[As]

(.36)**

(.14)*

Economic Need
(Detrended timber
prices)

[En]

(.52)*

(.03)*

(.12)†

(.73)*

(.13)*

(.02)*

Infanticide
(indictments)

[In]

R² = .87

Maternal
Asocialization
(bastardy)

[Ma]

(.31)*

(.34)*

Introjective Stress
(prostitution)

[Is]

(.94)**

*Path coefficients, $P_{i, j}$

**Exogenous effect,
= $\sqrt{1-R^2}$

†Non-Causative correlation,
= $(P_{As, En}) \times (P_{Is, En}) + (P_{As, Ma}) \times (P_{Is, Ma})$

filters of aggressive and introjective stress. The correlation of infanticide and asocialization, r_{In}, r_{Ma}, decomposes into $P_{In, Ma} + P_{Is, Ma} (P_{In, Is}) + P_{As, Ma} (P_{In, As})$, the direct and indirect paths. It is equal to .51. The dysfunctionality of asocialization—of confronting and disobeying ruling norms on sexual behavior—could lead to murderous acts against others or against oneself. Both of the latter may involve infan-

ticidal rage. Economic need has a much less decided effect
upon infanticide; explaining, perhaps, why so many poor,
unwed mothers did not dispose of their children in time of
want. Infanticide for the murdering parent was not an act
of necessity, but a response to stress.

One last set of steps remains: to discuss the model as a
whole. First, how much variation in each variable does the
path model explain? This is the R^2 figure, and the model
has high final R^2. It is conceivable, as noted above, that the
final R^2 for infanticide may be more a product of the magistrates' simultaneous concern for prosecution of certain
crimes along with infanticide, than for the causal relationships posited, but even this possibility points the way to a
fruitful area of research. Second, one can examine the size
of the path coefficients to see if they seem powerful enough
for inclusion in the model. In part, this was done when indicators were selected, insuring that the final multiple
regression would give sufficiently high beta weights to fit
this criterion of a successful model.

The path model was revised to examine the causes of
infanticide in eighteenth-century England. The indicators
chosen to represent the four variables of aggressive stress,
introjective stress, economic need, and material asocialization all appear in Chapter 5. While in every case, except
infanticide indictments, the dependent variable, these indicators differ from the seventeenth-century example, the
large theoretical model remains the same, as does the path
diagram. Witchcraft prosecutions decreased early in the
eighteenth century, and bastardy cases became the purview
of magistrates' courts, whose records are poorly preserved.
Murder and manslaughter indictments were therefore sub-
stituted for witchcraft cases. This is not an entirely acceptable solution, because the former were primarily crimes by
men against men. Bastardy prosecutions were replaced with
overlaying statistics, available for London and the outparishes in the Bills of Mortality. Timber prices were replaced
by real wages. Suicide rates, a direct measure of introjective
stress, were used instead of prostitution cases. In Chapter

5, the slopes of some of these indicators changed from negative to positive, or vice versa, when we shifted our inquiry from the beginning of the 18th century to its last decades. For this reason, two path diagrams were prepared, one for each period. There are a number of anomalies in diagram A3.2. Real wage increases should have a negative influence on infanticide, but instead show infanticide rising as real wages rose. Introjective stress strongly influenced infanticide, but again with a theoretically incorrect slope. Wage and suicide data was recorded without sex categories, making precise analysis difficult. Men dominated the former category, and the sex composition of the latter cannot be determined. Male suspects of infanticide were so few in number in relation to the women, that statistical comparisons of male wages and suicides might lose much of their force. Maternal asocialization and aggressive stress are strongly and positively correlated with infanticide, because

Path Diagram A3.2
Tentative Causes of Infanticide
in Middlesex, 1707 - 1727

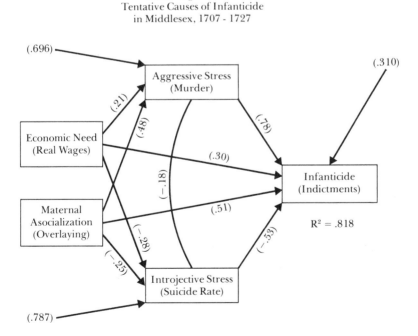

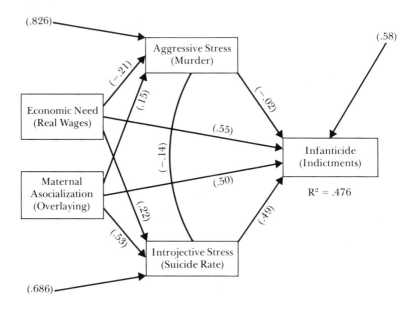

Path Diagram A3.3
Tentative Causes of Infanticide
in Middlesex, 1764 - 1784

overlaying was a woman's crime, and the number of murder of adults' indictments was falling for other reasons than
those related to stress. One more consideration is in order
about the diagram A3.2: it does not show the effects of
modernization. It is similar instead to the pattern of causes
discovered in path diagram A3.1, for the previous century.
This changes visibly in path diagram A3.3. Once again, real
wages does not describe the condition of women in domestic service or other lower class female pursuits. Changes in
the diagram of greater interest are the reversal of the introjective and the aggressive stress indicators. In the second
half of the 18th century, suicide was declining but murder
had reached a stable level, with the result that suicide rates
and infanticide indictment rates showed a strong and positive relationship, but murder ceased to measure changes in
aggressive stress levels. It is in the area of sentiment, of feeling, that the strongest indicators of infanticidal potential are

now found—in asocialization and introjective stress. This is an important result, for it was the feelings of mothers in this era of burgeoning sentimentality that determined their relationships to their newborns and older children. In modern nuclear domestic situations, this is what one would expect. The reduction in the final R^2 can be attributed to the difficulty of precisely measuring such subtle changes in sentiment.

Appendix 4

Indictment Rates in Middlesex, England, and the Colony of Massachusetts Bay, 1670-1780

The indictment rate for infanticide cases in Massachusetts courts is continuously and markedly higher than those of Middlesex English courts. Table A4.1 shows a 2.15 times higher average rate in Massachusetts than in Middlesex, England.

Table A4.1
Rates of Indictment for Infanticide, Massachusetts and
Middlesex, England, 1670–1780. (per hundred thousand) [a]

Period	Massachusetts	Middlesex (England)
1671–1700	1.41	.571
1701–1730	.775	.342
1731–1760	.475	.283
1761–1780	.181	.121

[a] Population calculated on the average at the middle of the period.

Rates of indictments do not, of course, measure rates of crime, but the difference between the apparently law-abiding Old World and the criminally inclined New World merits comment. The disparity seems the greater for the choice of the two jurisdictions. Supposedly wicked London, the graveyard of England, sat at the center of Middlesex. It was in London that the first foundling hospital opened its doors as a refuge for the multitudes of abandoned babies in the city's streets. Puritan Massachusetts, in contrast, was to be a sanctuary of law and order, no less than piety. Chapter 4 indicated that the pattern of commission and prosecution for the crime in both places was substantially the same. The differences were predictable, and do not require extensive explanation. How then may one explain the discrepancy in indictment rates? The answer appears throughout this essay, and is restated in the very paradox above. Puritan Massachusetts inquired into the behavior of its residents with suspicious perseverance. Little of serious importance escaped the eyes and ears of the magistrates. Much, on the contrary, could be hidden from the overworked parish officers, coroners, and magistrates of teeming London and its exploding outparishes. One should note that the two rates converged as time passed. As conditions in New England and England simultaneously progressed toward commercial heterogeneity, the disparity in infanticide indictment rates grew smaller.

Appendix 5

The London Bills of Mortality

The London bills of mortality remain an exasperating, enticing source of social and medical history and demography. The intention in this book was to employ them as a guide into regions where no other source could go. The reader may expect a fuller recounting of the actual numbers in the yearly summaries than offered in Chapter 5. This is given below.

Table A5.1
London Bills of Mortality *a* 1707–1727

Date	The Number Christened	The Number Buried	Some Causes of Death				
			Stillborn *b*	Infants *c*	Overlaid	Childbed *d*	Suicide
1707	16066	21600	547	88	68	258	38
1708	15862	21291	659	92	53	247	28
1709	15220	21800	619	83	41	215	36
1710	14928	24620	576	112	51	217	33
1711	14706	19833	573	77	37	195	26
1712	15660	21198	510	85	41	207	24
1713	15927	21057	567	88	44	178	34
1714	17495	26569	640	73	46	309	34
1715	17234	22232	531	52	47	275	28
1716	17421	24436	675	46	59	229	28
1717	18475	23446	685	54	70	243	37
1718	18307	26523	695	72	76	263	31
1719	18413	28347	670	68	67	292	26
1720	17479	25454	694	70	69	260	27
1721	18370	26142	728	73	67	299	52
1722	18339	25750	784	70	76	293	41
1723	19203	29197	778	86	88	291	45
1724	19370	25952	767	55	89	247	38
1725	18859	25523	711	55	71	263	59
1726	18808	29647	682	?	67	245	59
1727	18252	28418	590	?	86	221	47

a Source: *A Collection of the Yearly Bills of Mortality, 1657–1758* (London, 1759).
b Includes category "abortive."
c Includes category "chrysoms" (0–6 months) infant death.
d Does not include category "miscarriage," as these are very few, obviously very underreported, and only appear between 1723 and 1727.

Table A5.2
London Bills of Mortality ^a 1764–1784

Date	*The Number Christened*	*The Number Buried*	Some Causes of Death				
			Stillborn ^b	*Infants* ^c	*Overlaid*	*Childbed*	*Suicide*
1764	16801	23202	729	7673	10	231	33
1765	16374	23230	758	8073	4	249	54
1766	16257	23911	708	8035	2	199	42
1767	15980	22612	737	7668	3	174	37
1768	16042	23639	700	8229	11	207	31
1769	16714	21847	709	8016	4	185	28
1770	17109	22434	715	7994	6	270	32
1771	17072	21780	696	7617	8	172	34
1772	17916	26053	778	9112	10	194	47
1773	16805	21656	714	6850	4	192	33
1774	16998	20884	518	7742	4	203	22
1775	17629	20514	592	7596	4	188	29
1776	17280	19048	513	6857	8	193	32
1777	18300	23334	530	8889	4	222	37
1778	17300	20399	550	7355	2	175	45
1779	16769	20420	511	7261	1	209	28
1780	16634	20517	544	6810	2	190	34
1781	17026	20709	581	7083	2	209	26
1782	17101	17918	566	5320	2	140	25
1783	17091	19029	636	6632	3	144	26
1784	17179	17828	528	5729	0	133	23

^aSource: The Company of Parish Clerks of London, *A General Bill of All the Christenings & Burials . . . 1764–1803* British Library Folio 1877.e.1
^bIncludes category of "abortive."
^cIncludes category of "chrysoms" (0–2) infant death.

Notes

CHAPTER 1

[1] Marvin Harris, *Cannibals and Kings, the Origins of Cultures* (New York, 1977), 15; E. A. Wrigley, *Population and History* (New York, 1969), 42–43; William A. Langer, "Infanticide, A Historical Survey," *History of Childhood Quarterly* I (Winter, 1974), 353–366.

[2] R. H. Helmholz, "Infanticide in the Province of Canterbury During the Fifteenth Century," *HCQ* 2 (Winter 1975), 382–383; *Before the Bawdy Court, Selections from Church Court Records, 1300–1800* (Paul Hair, ed., London, 1972), 96, 103, 121–122.

[3] *Crown Pleas of the Wiltshire Eyre, 1249* (C.A.F, Meekings ed., Gateshead on Tyne, England, 1961), 189; *The Assizes Held at Cambridge, A.D. 1260* (W. M. Palmer ed., Linton, England, 1930, 3; Barbara Hanawalt, "The Female Felon in Fourteenth-Century England," *Viator* 5 (1974), 259–261.

[4] Barbara Hanawalt, *Crime and Conflict in English Communities, 1300–1348* (Cambridge, Mass., 1979), 154–157.

[5] James B. Given, *Society and Homicide in Thirteenth Century England* (Stanford, 1977), 36; *The 1253 Surrey Eyre* (C.A.F. Meekings and David Crook eds. [Surrey Record Society, 31], Guildford England, 1979), 107. On the coroners, see R. F. Hunnisett, *The Medieval Coroner* (Cambridge, England 1961), 121.

[6] Langer, "Infanticide" 356; Richard C. Trexler, "Infanticide in Florence: New Sources and First Results," *HCQ* I (Summer 1973) 104; Geneva data courtesy of Prof. William Monter, Northwestern University.

[7] Samuel E. Thorne, ed. and trans., *Bracton on the Laws and Customs of England,* 4v. (Cambridge, Mass., 1968–1976), II, 341; H. G. Richardson and G. O. Sayles, eds and trans., *Fleta, Volume II, Prologue, Book I, Book II* (London, 1955), 60–61; Marowe, "De Pace Terre and Ecclesie and Conseruacione Eiusdem . . ." (1503),

published in Bertha H. Putnam, *Early Treatises on the Practice of the Justices of the Peace in the Fifteenth and Sixteenth Centuries* (Oxford, 1924), 379; William Stanford, *Les Plees del Coron* (London, 1557), 21. The other major treatises of this century, Fitzherbert's own *L'Office* (London, 1538) and William Lambard's *Eirenarcha* (London, 1582) did not offer any new commentary, despite the fact that murder was a crime of some interest to the jurists; see Bertha H. Putnam, *Proceedings Before the Justices of the Peace in the Fourteenth and Fifteenth Centuries, Edward III to Richard III* (London, 1938), xxiii, cxlvi.

[8] Crompton, *L'Office* . . . (London, 1584), 194; James Dyer, *Reports of Cases in the Reigns of Henry VIII, Edward VI, Queen Mary and Queen Elizabeth* (John Vaillant ed. and trans., London, 1794) II, 186. On the debate over the meaning of murder and manslaughter, see J. M. Kaye, "The Early History of Murder and Manslaughter," *Law Quarterly Review* 83 (July and October 1967), 588–589 especially.

[9] *Calendar of Assize Records, Hertfordshire Assizes, Indictments, Elizabeth I, 1573–1603, James I, 1603–1625* 2v. *Assize Records, Sussex Indictments, Elizabeth I, James I,* 2v. (J. S. Cockburn ed., London, 1975–1976); *Assize Records, Essex Indictments, Elizabeth I* (Cockburn ed., London, 1978); Essex County Record Office Typescript "Calendar of Essex Assize Files, 1603–1714," Chelmsford, Essex; *Middlesex County Records, Indictments* . . . 2v. (John Cordy Jeaffreson ed., London, 1886–1887); *Calendar to the Sessions Records . . . 1613–1618,* New Series, 4v. (William Le Hardy ed., London, 1935–1941); Greater London [Middlesex] Record Office Typescript "Calendar of Sessions and Gaol Delivery Records, 1607–1612," London.

[10] Richard Crompton, *L'Office et Aucthoritie de Justicies de Peace* (2d. ed., London, 1593), 23. On Crompton see *L'Office et Aucthoritie* . . . (P. R. Glazebrook ed. [1584], London, 1972), iii–x, and C. W. Sutton, "Richard Crompton," *Dictionary of National Biography* (London, 1888), XIII, 148. For the contemporary reputation of Crompton's edition of *L'office,* see Ferdinando Pulton, *De Pace Regis et Regni* (London, 1609), preface, and William Dugdale, *Origines Juridiciales, or, Historical Memorials of the English Courts of Justice* . . . (London, 1680), 60–63. On rules of evidence, see John H. Langbein, *Torture and the Law of Proof, Europe and England in the Ancien Regime* (Chicago, 1976), 77–79 and after.

[11] Thomas R. Forbes, *Chronicle From Aldgate, Life and Death in Shakespeare's London* (New Haven, 1971), 172; J.D.J. Harvard, *The Detection of Secret Homicide* (London, 1960), 5–6; J. S. Cockburn, *A History of the English Assizes, 1558–1714* (Cambridge, England, 1972), 98.

[12] Hilles' case, March 11, 1568, Essex assize [Files] 35/10/2; Lawrence's case, March 8, 1571, Essex assize 35/13/1; Bond's case, July 30, 1576, Essex assize 35/22/10.

[13] Sir James Astry, *A General Charge to All Grand Juries* (London, 1725), 24; Tacke's case, May 11, 1615, Le Hardy, ed., *Calendar to the Sessions Records, Middlesex,* II, 329; Cooke's case, February 6, 1616; *Calendar to the Sessions Records, Middlesex,* III 168–169. A recent case of a mother delivering without prior knowledge of pregnancy appears in *South Bend [Indiana] Tribune* (December 7, 1977), p. 17.

[14] Crompton, *L'Office* . . . (London, 1606), 24.

[15] John Downame, *The Christian Warfare* (London, 1604), 39, 101–104; Hannibal Gamon, *Gods Smiting to Amendment* . . . (London, 1628), 28; William Perkins, *The Whole Treatise of the Case of Conscience* (c. 1596) in *William Perkins, 1558–1602* (Thomas F. Merrill ed., The Hague, 1966), 106–107 and after; William Gouge, *Of Domestical Duties* (London, 1602), 499–500; Samuel Burton, *A Sermon Preached at the General Assizes in Warwick* (London, 1620), 12–13.

[16] See William S. Holdsworth, *A History of English Law* (Boston, 1931), I, 588–589, 597. Ralph Houlbrooke, *Church Courts and the People During The English Reformation, 1520–1570* (Oxford, England, 1979), 79, indicates that the church courts were losing their effectiveness as punishers of incontinence in the last of these years, throwing even more of the burden upon civil authorities.

[17] Paul A. Slack, "Vagrants and Vagrancy in England," *Economic History Review*, 2d series, 27 (August 1974), 360; William Harrison, "The Description of Britain" [1577] in *Elizabethan England* (Lothrop Withington ed., London, 1876), 128; Carl Bridenbaugh, *Vexed and Troubled Englishmen, 1590–1642* (rev. ed., New York, 1976), 375. The immense increase in vagrancy in London is discussed in A. L. Beier, "Social Problems in Elizabethan England," *Journal of Interdisciplinary History*, 9 (Autumn, 1978), 203–222. There is some evidence that officials' connection of promiscuity with poverty may be sound; see Clark E. Vincent, "Familial and Generation Patterns of Illegitimacy," *Journal of Marriage and the Family* 31 (November, 1969), 662.

[18] The "personal conduct" statutes flooding the quarter sessions are discussed in Joan R. Kent, "Attitudes of Members of the House of Commons to the Regulation of 'Personal Conduct' in Late Elizabethan and Early Stuart England," *Bulletin of the Institute of Historical Research* XLVI (May, 1973), 41–71.

[19] 18 Eliz. I, c. 3 (1576); 7 James I, c. 4, (1609).

[20] William Lambard, "Charge to the Quarter Session After Easter, 1586," and Lambard, "An Ephemeris," in *William Lambard and Local Government* (Conyers Read ed., Ithaca, 1962), 85, 30; Thomas G. Barnes, *Somerset 1625–1640, A County's Government During the 'Personal Rule'* (Cambridge, Mass., 1961), 62; Peter Laslett, *The World We Have Lost* (New York, 1965), 135. On bastardy court cases see also J. S. Furley, *Quarter Session Government in Hampshire in the Seventeenth Century* (Winchester, 1937), 70–71, and *Minutes of Proceedings in Quarter Sessions . . . in the County of Lincoln* (S. A. Peyton ed., Lincoln, 1931), cix.

[21] Cheveley's case appears in "Calendar of Essex Quarter Sessions Records," IX, 2, 13, 116, 206.

[22] "Calendar, Essex Quarter Sessions," XV, 122–128 (April 2, May 22, 1589).

[23] For a poignant, popular rendition of this tragic process, see the entries in *English and Scottish Ballads* (Frances James Child ed., Boston, 1864), II, 265–266.

[24] Peter Spufford, "Population Movement in Seventeenth-Century England," *Local Population Studies*, 4 (1970), 41–50; A. F. J. Brown, *Essex in History* (London, 1977), 137. On property crimes at the Elizabethan and Stuart assizes, see Cockburn, "The Nature and Incidence of Crime in England, 1559–1625" in *Crime in England, 1550–1800* (Cockburn, ed., London, 1977) 68, 69.

[25] Citation of the kite case appears in Michael Dalton, *The Countrey Justice* (London, 1619), 218. See also J. Bond, *A Compleat Guide for Justices of Peace* (rev. ed., London, 1707), 141; *Burns Justice of the Peace and Parish Officer, Corrected and Greatly Enlarged* (London, 1845), 809; Sir Matthew Hale, *Pleas of the Crown* (London, 1682), 53; William Blackstone, *Commentaries on the Laws of England, Book the Fourth* (Oxford, 1769), 198; William Hawkins, *A Treatise of the Pleas of the Crown*, I (8th ed., London, 1824), 92, and Sir James F. Stephen, *A Digest of the Criminal Law* (London, 1877), fn. 1, 146.

[26] 21 James I, c. 27 (1624). The text used here is *Statutes at Large*, VII, ed., Danby Pickering (Cambridge, 1763), 298. The German imperial criminal code of 1532, the Carolina, also made provision for "maidens" (spinsters in England) suspected of secretly having and killing newborns. The accused were to be tortured

if they would not confess to the deed. Suspicion fell on those women "of whom such a suspected crime could be believed"; a notion equivalent to the presumption of guilt in 21 James I. c. 27. See John H. Langbein, *Prosecuting Crime in the Renaissance* (Cambridge, Mass., 1974), 277. The procedure was laid out in articles 35 and 36 of the Carolina.

[27] Keith Wrightson, "Infanticide in Earlier Seventeenth-Century England," *Local Population Studies*, 15 (1975), 19; Norman G. Brett-James, *The Growth of Stuart London* (London, 1966); Joel Samaha, *Law and Order in Historical Perspective, the Case of Elizabethan Essex*, (New York, 1973), 115. On the long tenure of assize justices see Cockburn, *English Assizes*, 57. P. E. H. Hair, using Jeaffreson's indictment figures, arrives at a much smaller rate, but the seven cases recorded for the years 1558–1603 must be too low, a result of the editor's selection process. See Hair, "Homicide, Infanticide, and Child Assault in the Late Tudor Middlesex," *LPS* 9 (1972), 44.

[28] *Journals of the House of Commons*, I, Session of 1623–1624, 769, 778–779, 793, 796. The bill against drunkenness had a very similar reading committee, see *CJ*, I (February 21, 1624), 674. On the Puritans in parliament, see Robert E. Ruigh, *The Parliament of 1624, Politics and Foreign Policy* (Cambridge, Mass., 1971), especially 159, and Patrick Collinson, *The Elizabethan Puritan Movement* (Berkeley, 1967), 54. See *CJ*, I, 368, 370, 421, 429 on earlier readings of the bill. On the underlying sexual fears of the Puritan party, see William Saffady, "Fears of Sexual License During the English Reformation," *HCQ* 1 (Summer, 1973), 89–97.

[29] *Essex Indictments*, Cockburn ed., and "Calendar of Essex Assize," I–II, 1603–1624, and III, 1625–1648.

[30] Kelyng, (1662), quoted in Leon Radzinowicz, *A History of the English Criminal Law and its Administration from 1750, I: The Movement for Reform*, 3v. (London, 1948), 431.

[31] Zachary Babington, *Advice to the Grand Jury in Cases of Blood* (London, 1673), 173. Blackstone, *Commentaries on the Laws of England, Book the Fourth*, 198; Radzinowicz, *A History of English Criminal Law*, I, 430. On North, see J. M. Kaye, "The Early History of Murder and Manslaughter," *Law Quarterly Review* 83 (July and October 1967), 588–589; Charles M. Radding, "The Evolution of Medieval Mentalities: A Cognitive Structure Approach," *American Historical Review* 83 (June 1978), 586, and Sir Frederick Pollock and F. W. Maitland, *The History of English Law* (2d. ed., Cambridge, England, 1968), II, 486. Dalton, *The Countrey Justice*, 277.

The development of the English Law was not unique. Early medieval Nordic law specified that only concealment of infanticide was a crime; confessions sufficed as punishment. See Juha Pentikainen, *The Nordic Dead-Child Tradition* (Helsinki, 1968), 83. Thereafter Scandinavian law seemed to follow the same course as the English. An awakened interest in the crime in the sixteenth century was followed by new statutes prescribing death for it, and in 1655 an act paralleling 21 James I, c. 27 was passed. See Pentikainen, *Dead-child Tradition*, 96–97.

[32] Michael Zuckerman, "The Fabrication of Identity in Early America," *William and Mary Quarterly*, 3rd series, 34 (April, 1977), 193. Crewe's case, July 10, 1612, Middlesex Sessions and Gaol Delivery Calendar, 52. Collyns' cases, June, 1565 Essex quarter sessions calendar, II, 1; July 21, 1564, Essex assize 35/61/5.

On the transformation of English agriculture in this era, see M. K. Ashby, *The Changing English Village* (Kineton, Warwickshire, 1974), 167, Eric Kerridge, *The Agricultural Revolution* (New York, 1967), passim, and Harold Peake, *The English Village, The Origin and Decay of Its Community* (London, 1922), 168–169 and after.

[33] Richard Trexler, "Infanticide in Florence," 105; see also Gregory Zilboorg, *A History of Medical Psychology* (reprinted, New York, 1967), 161. On the characterization of witches in folklore, literature and official commentary on the laws, see George Lyman Kittredge, *Witchcraft in Old and New England* (New York, 1958), 247 and passim, and Wallace Notestein, *A History of Witchcaft in England* (Washington, D.C.,1911), 41, 44–45 and after.

[34] For witchcraft indictments, see C. L'Estrange Ewen, *Witch Hunting and Witch Trials* (London, 1929), A. D. J. Macfarlane, "Witchcraft in Tudor and Stuart Essex," in *Crime in England, 1550–1800*) 79 (J. S. Cockburn ed.), and *Middlesex Sessions*, 4v. (Le Hardy ed.), I–IV.

[35] Macfarlane, *Witchcraft in Tudor and Stuart England* (New York, 1970), 244–249; Robert A. Levine, *Culture, Behavior, and Personality* (Chicago, 1973), 256–267. On the labelling of deviance, see Howard Becker, *The Other Side, Perspectives on Deviance* (New York, 1964), introduction, and Robert A. Dentler and Kai T. Erikson, "The Functions of Deviance in Groups," *Social Problems* 7 (Fall, 1959), 98–107.

CHAPTER 2

[1] John Winthrop, "A Model of Christian Charity" (1630) in *The Puritans*, 2v. (Perry Miller and Thomas H. Johnson eds., rev. ed., New York, 1963), I, 198. The Indians practiced infanticide, and the first English settlers were horrified. See Harold Driver, *The Indians of North America* (Chicago, 1964), 435–436 and John Winslow, *Good Newes From New England* (London, 1624), 55.

[2] T. H. Breen, "Presistent Localism: English Social Change and the Shaping of New England Institutions," *William & Mary Quarterly*, 3rd Series, 32 (January, 1975), 20–21; Michael Zuckerman, "The Fabrication of Identity in Early America," 199. There were fewer servants in New England than in England; see Abbot Emerson Smith, *Colonists in Bondage* ([1947] New York, 1971), 315–317, and Laslett, *The World We Have Lost*, 65 and after. Until the end of the seventeenth century, New England men notably outnumbered New England women; See John Demos, *A Little Commonwealth, Family Life in Plymouth Colony* (New York, 1970), 77; Daniel Scott Smith, "The Demographic History of Colonial New England," *Journal of Economic History* 32 (March, 1972), 197, and Rudy Seward, "The Colonial Family in America," *Journal Of Marriage & Family* 35 (February, 1973), 65. The standard work is Herbert Moller, "Sex Composition and Correlated Culture Patterns of Colonial America," *William and Mary Quarterly*, 3rd series, 2 (October, 1945), 113–153.

[3] Perry Miller, "Puritan State and Puritan Society," in Miller, *Errand Into the Wilderness* ([1956] New York, 1964), 143; Edward Taylor, cited in Roger Thompson, *Women in Stuart England and America* (London, 1974), 10; Edmund S. Morgan, *The Puritan Family: Religion and Domestic Relations in Seventeenth Century New England* (rev. ed., New York, 1966), 43; Demos, *A Little Commonwealth*, 128–144; *The Puritans* (Perry Miller and Thomas H. Johnson, eds.,), II, 696.

[4] The literature of the reception of English law is immense. See David Flaherty, "Introduction," *Essays in the History of Early American Law* (Chapel Hill, 1969), 8–14, as well as Zechariah Chafee, Jr., "Colonial Courts and the Common Law," *Proceedings of the Massachusetts Historical Society* LXVIII (October 1944), 132–159, and Julius Goebel, Jr., "King's Law and Local Custom in 17th Century New England" *Columbia Law Review* 31 (1931), 416–448. See also Carol F. Lee, "Discretion-

ary Justice in Early Massachusetts," *Essex Institute Historical Collections* 112 (April, 1976), 139. Despite demands for reform of the English discretionary system, partially answered by codification of the criminal law in New England, the magistrates in the colonies continued to exercise great power in administration of the law.

⁵Bradley Chapin, "Criminal Law in Colonial America 1609–1660," 2; ms. in possession of the author. Proof of this proposition lies in the 1647 Rhode Island code, whose captions all refer to the statutes in Dalton's *Countrey Justice*. See also Joseph H. Smith, *Colonial Justice in Western Massachusetts, 1639–1702, the Pynchon Court Record* (Cambridge, Mass., 1961), 146–147.

⁶*The Laws & Liberties of Massachusetts* [1648] (Max Farrand ed., Cambridge, Mass. 1929), 5; Edwin Powers, *Crime and Punishment in Early Massachusetts, 1620–1692* (Boston, 1966), 259.

⁷*Public Records of the Colony of Connecticut* I (Hammond Trumbull, ed., Hartford, 1850), 77, 539; VI, 144; David Pulsifer, ed., *Records of the Colony of New Plymouth in New England, Laws: 1623–1682* (David Pulsifer ed., Boston, 1861), 12; Joseph H. Smith, "The English Common Law in Early America," *The English Legal System: Carryover to the Colonies* (Los Angeles, 1975), 26–27.

⁸Edward Coke, *The Third Part of the Institutes of the Laws of England* (4th ed., London, 1669), 48. On the Bible as a supportive source of law in New England, see George L. Haskins, *Law and Authority in Early Massachusetts* (New York, 1960), 148–149.

⁹The Massachusetts cases are drawn from the Records and Minute Books of the Massachusetts superior court of judicature (SCJ), 1692–1780; file papers of the SCJ in the "Court Files, Suffolk, [and etc.]" the special courts [records], 1686–1687, all at the New Suffolk county court house, Boston, as well as John Noble, et al., eds., *Records of the Court of Assistants of the Colony of Massachusetts Bay*, 3v. (Boston, 1901–1928). Connecticut cases were drawn from the records of the court of assistants of Connecticut 1665–1711; superior court records, 1711–1780, and the Crimes and Misdemeanors, 1st & 2nd Series, 1665–1808, and the file papers of the high courts of criminal jurisdiction, Connecticut state library, Hartford.

¹⁰In 1692, the general court of Massachusetts included the Jacobean infanticide law of 1624 in a revised code of capital offenses but the code was disallowed by the privy council in 1695. The general court reenacted the infanticide law in December 1696: see *Acts and Resolves of . . . Massachusetts* (Boston, 1869), I, 55 (1692), 255 (1696). For the Connecticut law, see *Acts and Laws Passed by the General Assembly [of Connecticut]*, May 1699, in *Public Records of the Colony of Connecticut, From August to May 1706* (Charles J. Hoadley ed., Hartford, 1868), 285. The editor notes that the law was copied from the Massachusetts statute, not the English statute itself.

¹¹John Winthrop, *Journal* [*History of New England*]; *Original Narratives of Early American History, vs. 18–19* (James K. Hosmer ed., New York, 1908), xvix, 282–283.

¹²*Records of the Court of Assistants*, II (1904), 78.

¹³*Records of the Court of Assistants*, II (1904), 70, 108, 126; *Records of the First Church in Boston* (Richard D. Pearce ed. [Publications of the Colonial Society of Massachusetts, 39] Boston, 1961), 38; *Province and Court Record of Maine*, I (Portland, 1928), 100; *The Diary of Samuel Sewall*, 2 vol. [December 1, 1705] (M. Halsey Thomas ed., New York, 1973), I, 532.

¹⁴*Records of the Colony of New Plymouth in New England*, II, 132–1350.

¹⁵Winthrop, *Journal*, xvix, 317–318.

¹⁶On the use of the conviction rate in criminological studies, see Ted Robert Gurr, et al., *The Politics of Crime and Conflict* (Beverley Hills, Calif., 1977), 19.

¹⁷For the Maryland cases, *Archives of Maryland* (William H. Browne et. al., eds. Baltimore, 1883–1965); see Volumes 10, 41, 53, 54, 57, 59, 60, 65, 66, for the infanticide cases for the period 1656 to 1676. Colledge's case [1673], *Archives of Maryland*, v. 57, 599. Colonial population statistics are drawn from [Bureau of the Census], *A Century of Population Growth* (Washington, D.C., 1909), 6–9. The Maryland figures are reduced by Russell Menard, "Immigrants and their Increases: The Process of Population Growth in Early Maryland," in *Law, Society & Politics in Early Maryland* (Aubrey C. Land *et al.*, eds., Baltimore, 1977), 88–110.

¹⁸For Brown's case June 23, 1691, May 8, 1693, see records of the court of assistants of Connecticut, 174–175, 193; Wyar's case 1709 appears in records of the superior court, for a superior court held at New London, p. 243. Hackleton's case, 1665, Crimes & Misdemeanors, I, 6, 7, 10–13; Briggs' case, 1668, Crimes and Misdemeanors, I, 32, 33. On the latter two cases see William K. Holdsworth, "Law and Society in Colonial Connecticut, 1636–1672" (Unpubl. Ph.D. thesis, Claremont Graduate School, 1974), 384.

¹⁹Frankling's Case [1643] cited in Robert Bremner, ed., *Children and Youth in America, A Documentary History I: 1600–1865* (Cambridge, Mass., 1970), 123. See also Latham's case, *Records of Plymouth Colony* (Nathaniel B. Surtleff ed., Boston, 1855), III, 71–71; Perry's case, *Winthrop's Journal*, xviii, 318; Bennetts' case, 1674, *Records of the Court of Assistants*, I (1901), 11; Chadwick's case, SCJ, "1710–1714" 67, 69–70.

On childrearing, see Joseph E. Illick, "Child-Rearing in 17th Century England and America," Lloyd Demause, ed., *The History of Childhood* (New York, 1974), 303–350, as well as Edward Shorter, *The Making of the Modern Family* (rev. ed., New York, 1977), 168–204, and David E. Stannard, "Death and the Puritan Child," *American Quarterly*, 26 (December, 1974), 463–464.

²⁰The theory that indictment for crimes reflects community biases is discussed in Chapter 1 above. Convictions may also be influenced in this fashion. Overall, the poor, the ethnic and racial minority member, and the isolated individual suffer disproportionately more in criminal justice systems than other, less socially disadvantaged groups. See Sue Titus Reid, *Crime and Criminology* (Hinsdale, Ill., 1977), 196–303, as well as David J. Rothman, *The Discovery of the Asylum* (Boston, 1971), 3–29.

²¹Linda Auwers, "Female Crime and Human Sin in A Colonial New England Community," read to the 1975 Berkshire Conference on Women's History, p. 3.; ms. in possession of the author. Moore's Case can be traced in "Crimes and Misdemeanors" I, 273–283. Threeneedles' case, SCJ, II, 199–200. On her family, see Sewell, *Diary*, I, 400.

²²On New England enslavement of blacks, see Winthrop Jordan, *White Over Black, American Attitudes Toward the Negro* [1968] (Baltimore, 1969), 66–71. New England treatment of the Indians is still a subject of controversy, see Alden Vaughan, *New England Frontier, Puritans & Indians 1620–1675* (rev. ed., New York, 1979), xvii. It should be noted that black defendants, male and female, were convicted twice as often for all murders as white defendants. The meaning of this fact is traced in N. E. H. Hull, "Female Felons: Women and Serious Crime in the High Courts of Colonial Massachusetts, 1673–1774" (Ph.D. diss., Columbia University, 1981), chapter four.

[23] On Anglicization of the law, see John M. Murrin, "The Legal Transformation, The Bench and Bar of 18th Century Massachusetts," in *Colonial America* (Stanley N. Katz, ed., Boston, 1971), 415–449, as well as Powers, *Crime and Punishment*, 303–308.

[24] Michael Wigglesworth, *The Diary of Michael Wigglesworth, 1653–1657* (Edmund S. Morgan ed., New York, 1965), 120, [Nov. 18, 1653]; Wigglesworth, "The Day of Doom" in *Seventeenth Century American Poetry* (Harrison T. Meserole ed., New York, 1968); see especially lines 101–102: "No hiding place, can from his face sinners at all conceal" 58; Thomas Shepard Jr. to Thomas Shepard III, in Miller and Johnson, eds., *The Puritans*, II, 719–720; *Records of the Suffolk County Court, 1671–1680*, Part I (Zechariah Chafee Jr. ed. [Collections of the Colonial Society of Massachusetts, 24] Boston, 1933), lxxxvii.

[25] Wigglesworth, December, 1654 *Diary*, 78 *Record of the Colony and Plantation of New Haven*, 2 v. (Charles J. Hoadley, ed., Hartford, 1857–1858), I, 233–239.

[26] Emmison's case, SCJ I, 50–51; file #2636, Suffolk court files, vol. 31, 95; Smith's case, file #3718, Suffolk court files, vol. 41, p. 76; Richardson's case, June 1, 1715 "Richmond County [Virginia], Fines, Examinations of Criminals, Tryalls of Slaves, 1710 to 1754," 12–13, Virginia State Library, Richmond.

[27] Anne Bradstreet, "The Flesh and the Spirit" in *American Poetry* (Meserole ed.), 21; *Massachusetts Laws and Liberties* [1648], 6; *Public Records of the Colony of Connecticut*, I, 77.

[28] "Extracts From the Records of York County," March 25th, 1636 *Collections of the Maine Historical Society*, (Portland, Me., 1865), I, 364–365; *Records of New Haven* I, 77–89; *Records of the Particular Court of the Colony of Connecticut* [1638–1649] *Connecticut Colonial Records*, I, 45, 78; *Records of the Court of Assistants*, II, 39–140. Powers, *Crime and Punishment*, 404–405, has tabulated the county indictments. See *Colonial Laws of Massachusetts, Reprinted from the Edition of 1660* (Boston, 1889), 257, for the bastardy statute. David Flaherty, *Privacy in Colonial New England* (Charlottesville, Va., 1972), argued that this moral regime was not so well enforced at the level of the constable and town watchman, but in trials for serious crimes it is apparent to us that prior sexual offenses had not gone unnoticed and were often used against a defendant.

[29] Wolfgang Lederer, *The Fear of Women* (New York, 1968), 208; John Demos, "Underlying Themes in the Witchcraft of Seventeenth Century New England" *American Historical Review*, 75 (1970), 1311–1326. For Parsons' case, see *Records of the Governor and Company of Massachusetts Bay*, 6v. (Nathaniel Shurtleff ed., Boston, 1853–1854), III, 229. Fuller's case appears in Samuel G. Drake, *Annals of Witchcraft in New England* [1869] (New York, 1967), 150–153. Glover's case is noted in Powers, *Crime and Punishment*, 461–462. Martha Emmison's case January 10, 1692 appears in Suffolk files, vol. 32, p. 31. This theme also forms the concluding chapter of Lyle Koehler's *A Search for Power, the Weaker Sex in Seventeenth-Century New England* (Urbana, Ill., 1980).

[30] Data on the Salem witches is taken from Demos, "Witchcraft," Chadwich Hansen, *Witchcraft at Salem* (New York, 1969), 126, 137, and Powers, *Crime and Punishment*, 459–468.

Perry Miller, *The New England Mind, from Colony to Province* ([1953] Boston, 1961), 209, finds the witchcraft episode "peripheral" to the larger dilemma: "How, under the terms of the new charter, could [Puritan New England] survive the disintegrating and seemingly irresistible consequences of the Half-way Covenant?"

But internecine contention among the ministerial fellowship and the loss of elective governorship in the new charter might well have led to "the need for scapegoats . . . no wonder Increase Mather returned in the spring of 1692 to find Salem jail full of witches," David S. Lovejoy, *The Glorious Revolution in America* (New York, 1972), 353, has argued.

[31] Cotton Mather, *Diary*, I, November 17, 1698; Mather, *Pillars of Salt, An History of Some Criminals Executed in This Land for Capital Crimes* (Boston, 1699), 3, 14–15, 20, 43, 60–61, 101–104, 106; John Williams, *Warning to the Unclean . . . Preached at Springfield Lecture, August 25, 1698, at the Execution of Sarah Smith* (Boston, 1699), 4, 6, 12, 15, 17, 22, 24, 30, 32, 42. On the execution sermon as a "jeremiad" see Ronald A. Bosco, "Lectures at the Pillory: The Early American Execution Sermon," *American Quarterly*, 30 (Summer, 1978), 156–176.

[32] Thomas Foxcroft, *Lessons of Caution for Young Sinners, A Sermon Preached on the Lord's Day, September 23, 1733 . . . with Mr. Byles' Conference with the Prisoner as She Walked to the Place of Execution . . .* (Boston, 1733), 7, 15, 33, 60, 61–68. Chamblit's case appears in SCJ, "1730–1733" and Suffolk files #35693, vol. 251, p. 125.

[33] Emmison's case, examinations and coroner's inquest, Suffolk County court files, file #2549–2668, vol. 34.

[34] Andrews' case, [March 10, 1696], SCJ, "1686–1700," II, 47, 49–50.

[35] Howland's case, [March 14, 1698], SCJ, "1686–1700," II, 235, 246–247.

[36] Munn's case, [May 5–19, 1699], records of the court of assistants and superior court [Connecticut] 291–293; Prosecution summation [?] Crimes and Misdemeanors, I, 223.

[37] *Public Records of the Colony of Connecticut, 1689–1706,* 285. The editor, C. J. Hoadley, noted "the immediate occasion of the passage of the act here was a recent case happening in Farmington", 285, that is, Munn's case.

[38] Robert Middlekauff, *The Mathers, Three Generations of Puritan Intellectuals 1596–1728* (New York, 1971), 349.

CHAPTER 3

[1] Joseph Addison, *The Guardian* (July 11, 1713); Daniel Defoe, *Augusta Triumphans* (London, 1728), 9; Jonathan Swift, *A Modest Proposal* (Dublin, 1729), 3. See also Thomas Coram, *An Account of the Hospital for the Maintenance and Education of Exposed and Deserted Young Children* (London, 1749), iii and after.

[2] *The Proceedings at the Sessions for London and Middlesex, Holden at the Old Bailey, Beginning on Wednesday, the Sixteenth of July, 1679,* 12. On the value of the OBSP see John H. Langbein, "The Criminal Trial before the Lawyers" *University of Chicago Law Review,* 45 (Winter, 1978), 263–316, and J. M. Beattie, "Crime in Surrey, 1733–1763" in *Crime in England, 1550–1800* (Cockburn ed.), 164–174. The OBSP used in this study were obtained at the Langdell Library, Harvard University, the Bodley Library, Oxford, the Guildhall Library, London, and the Library of Congress Law Library, Washington, D.C.

[3] Longworth's case, *OBSP,* January 16, 1685; Stooke's case, *OBSP,* January 17, 1685; Brown's case, *OBSP,* October 14, 1685; Philmore's case, *OBSP,* October 13, 1686; Trabern's case, *OBSP,* April 6, 1687; Jones' case, *OBSP,* January 13, 1688. Samuel Smith, Ordinary of the Newgate Prison, *OBSP,* October 17, 1687.

[4] Jewring's Case, January 1674 session (coroner's inquest December 17, 1673);

sessions papers, city of London quarter sessions of general gaol delivery, Corporation of London Records Office; Morris' case, *OBSP*, September 7, 1722; Hamby's case, *OBSP*, April 24, 1734.

[5] Parker's case, *OBSP*, April 10, 1717; Bateman's case, *OBSP*, February 27, 1723; Banestly's case, *OBSP*, August 30, 1721.

[6] Jones' case, *OBSP*, July 13, 1720; Haywood's case, Testimony by _____, sister at hospital where Haywood lay, November 3, 1762, sessions papers, city of London quarter sessions. Haywood at first denied the pregnancy, then denied any intention of losing the child.

In common law, only idiots and lunatics could gain pardon for their acts, and that only after conviction; temporary insanity was not a reason for a pardon, much less a defense that could lead to an acquittal until these infanticide cases arose. On insanity law, see Nigel Walker, *Crime and Insanity in England, I: The Historical Perspective* (Edinburgh, 1968), 125–137 and pages 146–147, Chapter 6.

[7] Spinton's case, *OBSP*, September 1771, 442–444; Curtis' case, *OBSP*, September 1784, 1221–1223; Langbein, "The Criminal Trial Before the Lawyers," 307–314.

[8] Clifton's case, *Whole Proceedings on the King's Commissions of Oyer and Terminer, and General Gaol Delivery, Held for the County of Surrey . . . March 1774* (London, 1774), 12–14; J. M. Beattie, "Women's Crime in Eighteenth-Century England," *Journal of Social History* 8 (Summer, 1975).

[9] "Calendar of Essex Assize files" Essex county record office, IV, 1684–1715. Judges could mitigate conviction when it occurred; for example in Mary Curtis's case, *Proceedings of the Assizes for the County of Essex . . . August 1741* (London, 1741), n.p.

[10] Jenning's case, SCJ "1771", June 16, 1771; Flora's case, SCJ, "1757–1759", 295–296; Patience's cases, SCJ, "1730–1733", 122–123, SCJ, "1733–1736", 228.

[11] Bond, *A Complete Guide for Justices of Peace, Revised, and Corrected . . .* (London, 1707), 141. Gilbert, *The Law of Evidence* (5th ed., Philadelphia, 1788), 268–269. Blackstone cited similar precedents, *Commentaries on the Laws of England, Book the Fourth,* 425, as did other commentators and manual writers including Hale, *Pleas of the Crown,* II, 288–289, Eden, *Principles of Penal Law,* (2d ed., London, 1771), 15–16, and later, Paley, *Principles of Moral and Political Philosophy* (London, 1817), 407.

[12] Curtis' case, *OBSP*, September, 1784.

[13] For example, Sarah Hunter's case, *OBSP*, July, 1769. The table is based on *Report from the Select Committee on the Criminal Laws; House of Commons to the House of Lords,* (July 8, 1820).

[14] Henry Fielding, *An Enquiry into the Causes of the Late Increase in Robbers* [1751] (London, 1930), 16. See also J. M. Beattie, "Towards A Study of Crime in 18th Century England: A Note on Indictments," in *The Triumph of Culture, Eighteenth Century Perspectives,* (Paul Fritz and David Williams eds., Toronto, 1972), 314.

[15] For the Surrey data, see J. M. Beattie, "The Pattern of Crime in England, 1660–1800," *Past and Present* 62 (February, 1974), 61. The Massachusetts population estimates are from *A Century of Population Growth,* 9. The Middlesex population data appears in Phyllis Deane and W. A. Cole, *British Economic Growth, 1669–1959* (2d ed., Cambridge, England, 1967), 103.

[16] Thomas R. Forbes, "Crowner's Quest" *Transactions of the American Philosophical Society,* 68, Part I, (1978), 40.

[17] William Wordsworth, "The Complaint of a Forsaken Indian Woman" [1798], *The Complete Poetical Works of William Wordsworth*, 10v. (Boston, 1911), II, 57, "The Prelude" (1799), *Complete Poetical Works*, III, 40.

[18] Lawrence Stone, *The Family, Sex, and Marriage in England, 1500–1800* (New York, 1977), especially 449–478, places the watershed of the affective nuclear domestic group's modernity at 1640. Thereafter, generations of children, themselves becoming parents, began to express warmth and affection for children more freely. Alice Ryerson, "Medical Advice on Childrearing, 1550–1900," *Harvard Educational Review* 41 (1961), finds 1750 the turning point in improvement of infant care advice.

[19] J. H. Plumb, "The New World of Children in Eighteenth-Century England," *Past and Present* 67 (May, 1975), 65; Ross W. Beales, "In Search of the Historical Child: Miniature Adulthood and Youth in Colonial New England," *American Quarterly* 27 (October, 1975), 396.

[20] David H. Flaherty, "Law and the Enforcement of Morals in Early America," *Perspectives in American History* 5 (1971), 250–251.

[21] "Calendar of Essex Quarter Session Records, 1685–1715" Essex county record office; Mansion House justice court, minute books of proceedings, 1785–1786, Corporation of London record office; Guildhall magistrates court, minute books, 1784–1785, Corporation of London records office; Middlesex quarter sessions of the peace, rolls and sessions papers, 1778–1780, Greater London record office. On premarital pregnancy rates, see Daniel S. Smith and Michael S. Hindus, "Premarital Pregnancy in America, 1640–1971: An Overview and Interpretation," *Journal of Interdisciplinary History* 5 (Spring 1975), 550; Edward Shorter, *The Making of the Modern Family*, 79–108, and Robert Wells, "Illegitimacy and Bridal Pregnancy in Colonial America," presented to the American Society for Eighteenth-Century Studies, Chicago, April 1978, 11–12.

[22] Grindall's case, *OBSP*, February 23, 1769; Harris' case, *OBSP*, May 1781. The new attitude made its way into literature; see, for example Wordsworth, "The Thorn" (1798), *Complete Poetical Works*, II, 18–27, lines 23–34, 67–77, 188–243; Sir Walter Scott, *The Heart of Midlothian* ([1819], London, 1906), especially 236–237; and George Eliot, *Adam Bede* (London, 1859), 302–303.

[23] *Parliamentary History of England, 17: 1771–1774* (London, 1813), 452–453.

Demand for an end to capital punishment for infanticide was also growing at this time in France, again upon a tide of both experience in the courts and enlarged sympathy for mothers; see Yvonne Bongert, "L'Infanticide Au Siècle de Lumières (Apropos d'un Ouvrage Recent)," *Revue Historique de Droit Francais et Etranger* (April–June 1978), 247–257.

[24] Blackstone, quoted in James Heath, *Eighteenth-Century Penal Theory* (Oxford, England, 1963), 191; Michael Foster, *A Report on Some Proceedings on the Commission of Oyer and Terminer . . . To Which are Added Discourses Upon the Crown Law* (Oxford, England, 1762), 305. On the late eighteenth-century reform movement, see Sir Leon Radzinowicz, *A History of the English Criminal Law I: The Movement for Reform*, particularly 430–434, for the parliamentary committee of 1770.

[25] See *Continuation of the Statutes at Large* (Cambridge, England, 1804), 205, for 43 Geo III, c. 58, section 3. Ellenborough's speech appears in *Parliamentary History of England* 36 (London, 1820), 1245–1247. On the passage of the bill, see *Journals of the House of Lords*, 44 (1802–1804), 11, 265, 286, and *Journals of the House of Commons*, 58 (1802–1803), 425, 509, 514, 516.

[26] Beaumont's case is in W. M. Medland and Charles Weobly, *A Collection of Remarkable and Interesting Criminal Trials* (London, 1803), 326–328.

[27] Thomas Starkie, *A Practical Treatise on the Laws of Evidence and Digest of Proofs in Civil and Criminal Proceedings*, 3v. (London, 1824), II, 964–949, 959; William O. Russell, *A Treatise on Crimes and Indictable Misdemeanors* 2v. (2d. ed., London, 1826–1828), I, 425, 439–440, 475–576; 477; Thomas Chitty, *Burns Justice of the Peace and Parish Officer* . . . *Corrected and Greatly Enlarged* . . . , 6v. (London, 1845), III, 810–811.

[28] Kirby's case, *OBSP*, April 11, 1804, 223; Smith's case, *OBSP*, July 4, 1804, 321–323; Dixon's case, *OBSP*, July 10, 1805, 421–423. The presiding judge at the sessions in Sarah Evans' case, *OBSP*, April 1, 1813, 201–210, instructed a jury that common fame for pregnancy was sufficient to disprove concealment. Here, notoriety for immorality worked to the defendant's advantage.

[29] *Annotated Laws of Massachusetts* 9, Chapter 272, section 22, 391–392; *Connecticut Laws and Statutes* IV, 68, 69. Durgin's case appears in the James Sullivan Papers, Boston Public Library, Ch. F. 11.100. The actual grand jury indictment deposited in the Sullivan papers was endorsed with the defendant's plea, the jury verdict, the sentence, and Sullivan's own note on the decision not to prosecute the accessories.

CHAPTER 4

[1] The historical use of criminal records is discussed in Ted Robert Gurr, Peter N. Grabosky, and Richard C. Hula, *The Politics of Crime and Conflict* (Beverly Hills, Calif., 1977), 3–34.

[2] There are dangers in overly credulous reading of these records; see J. S. Cockburn, "Early-Modern Assize Records as Historical Evidence," *Journal of the Society of Archivists* 5 (October, 1975), 215–231; Carol Z. Weiner, "Is A Spinster an Unmarried Woman?" *American Journal of Legal History* 20 (1976), 28–31; J. M. Beattie, "Towards a Study of Crime in Eighteenth-Century England, a Note on Indictments," 299–314, and Michael S. Hindus and Douglas L. Jones "Quantitative and Theoretical Approaches to the History of Crime and Law," Newberry Library Papers in Family and Community History, 77–4G (1977).

[3] Deposition of John Doleman, January 1646, Middlesex quarter sessions papers, Greater London record office; Dell's case is discussed in John Langbein, *Prosecuting Crime in the Renaissance*, 48; "The Children in the Wood" (ca. 1601), appears in Francis J. Child, *English and Scottish Ballads*, III, 135; on Austin, see *The Complete Newgate Calendar*, 5v. (G. T. Crook ed., London, 1926), II, 93.

[4] Peter Laslett, *The World We Have Lost*, 134. See also fn. 24, Chapter 5.

[5] On standardization, see H. T. Reynolds, *Analysis of Nominal Data* (Beverly Hills, 1977), 17–18.

[6] Ellyot's case, *Sussex Assizes* (Cockburn, ed.), I, 5, 43 (August 3, 1565; July 17, 1566); Linscale's case, *Depositions From the Castle of York, Relating to Offenses Committed in the Northern Counties* (James Raine, Jr. ed., London, 1861), 131–133, Farmer's case, *Sussex Assizes*, I, 219 (March 3, 1589); Mouser's case, *Sussex Assizes*, I, 225 (June 27, 1589).

[7] On female assault in Hertfordshire, see Carol Z. Wiener, "Sex Roles and Crime in Late Elizabethan Hertfordshire," *Journal of Social History* 8 (Summer, 1975), 45.

The Middlesex data are from *Middlesex Sessions Records* (LeHardy ed.), I–IV, passim.

⁸Thomas A. Green, "The Jury and the English Law of Homicide, 1200–1600," *Michigan Law Review* (1976), 415–497; Cockburn, *English Assizes*, 86–132; J. H. Baker, "Criminal Courts and Procedure at Common Law," in *Crime in England* (Cockburn, ed.), 32–45.

⁹Lambarde, *Eirenarcha*, 218; Thorowgood's cases, March 14, 1623; March 17, 1625, *Hertfordshire Assizes* (Cockburn ed.), II, 259, 285–286; Keith Wrightson, "Infanticide in Earlier Seventeenth-Century England," 13–14.

¹⁰Tyndall's case, March 18, 1594 Essex assize, 35/36/1; Payne's case, March 5, 1595 Essex assize 35/37/1; Carter's case, July 28, 1617 Essex assize, 35/59/1.

¹¹On the extent of English servitude, see Laslett and Wall, "England, the Median Household Size," in *Household and Family in Past Time* (Laslett and Wall eds., Cambridge, England, 1972), 56–57.

¹²Allen's case, *OBSP*, October 12, 1737; [James Guthrie], *Behavior, Confession, & Dying Words of the Malefactors who were Executed at Tyburn* . . . (London, 1739), 4. Not all of Newgate's prisoners were so cooperative; Agatha Ashbrook, convicted in 1708 of infanticide, refused to confide in the ordinary. See P. Linebaugh, "The Ordinary of Newate and his Account," in *Crime in England, 1550–1800* (Cockburn, ed.), 258.

CHAPTER 5

¹William L. Langer, "Infanticide: A Historical Survey," 353–365, and Thomas McKeown, *The Modern Rise of Population* (New York, 1976), 146, believe infanticide was widespread; in dissent are E. A. Wrigley, "Family Limitation in Pre-Industrial England," *Economic History Review* 19 (1967), 105 and Keith Wrightson, "Infanticide in Early Seventeenth Century England," 19.

²John Taylor, cited in Joan Thirsk, *The Agrarian History of England and Wales IV: 1500–1640* (Cambridge, 1967), 449.

³W. K. Jordan, *Philanthropy in England, 1480–1660* (London, 1959), appendix; J. S. Cockburn, "The Nature and Incidence of Crime in England 1559–1625, A Preliminary Survey" in *Crime in England* (Cockburn, ed.), 68–69.

⁴The economic data in these tables was obtained from appendices in *The Agrarian History of England and Wales, IV:1500–1640* (Joan Thirsk, ed.)

⁵Naroll, "A Tentative Index of Culture Stress," *International Journal of Social Psychiatry* 5 (1959), 107–116.

⁶Spufford, "Population Movement in Seventeenth-Century England," 41–50.

⁷From Joel Samaha, *Crime and Disorder in Historical Perspective*, tables at 125–127, one can gain a visual sense of this discrepancy.

⁸On the rough treatment given many children, see Chapter 2, fn. 19 and Chapter 6, fn. 8.

⁹See Austin L. Porterfield, "Indices of Suicide and Homicide by States and Cities: Some Southern and Non-Southern Contrasts with Implications for Research," *American Sociological Review* 14 (August, 1949), 481–490; Andrew F. Henry and James F. Short, Jr., *Suicide and Homicide* (Glencoe, Ill., 1954); Alex D. Pokorny, "Human Violence: A Comparison of Homicide, Aggravated Assault, Suicide, and Attempted Suicide," *Journal of Criminal Law, Criminology, and Police Science* 56 (1965).

[10] Emile Durkheim, *Suicide* (George Simpson ed., New York, 1951), 24–25; Helene Deutsche, *The Psychology of Women, A Psychoanalytic Interpretation* 2v. (rev. ed., New York, 1973), I, 269–176.

[11] See especially Phillip J. Resnick, "Murder of the Newborn: A Psychiatric Review of Neonaticide," *American Journal of Psychiatry*, 126 (April, 1970), 1414–1420, and Resnick, "Child Murder by Parents: A Psychiatric Review of Filicide," *American Journal of Psychiatry* 125 (September, 1969), 77–78.

[12] On the underreporting of suicide, see Thomas R. Forbes, *Chronicle from Aldgate, Life and Death in Shakespeare's London* (New Haven, 1971), 31.

[13] April E. Ahlers, "The Whole Duty of an Englishwoman, 1700–1792" (Ph.D. thesis, Tulane University), 1974, 98–139. An antique proof of the dominance of these values is Mrs. Sarah S. Ellis, *The Women of England, Their Social Duties, and Domestic Habits* (London, 1839), passim.

[14] P. E. H. Hair, "Bridal Pregnancy in Rural England in Earlier Centuries," *Population Studies* 20 (November, 1966), 237; Peter Laslett and Karla Ovsterveen, "Long Term Trends in Bastardy in England," *Population Studies* 27 (July, 1973, 260.

[15] David Levine and Keith Wrightson, *Poverty and Piety in an English Village, Terling, 1525–1700* (New York, 1979), 132–133.

[16] M. Dorothy George, *London Life in the Eighteenth Century* ([1931] reprinted London, 1951), 3; English mortality rates from Deane and Cole, *British Economic Growth*, 12; see also P. E. Razzell, "Population Change in 18th Century England: A Reinterpretation," *Economic History Review* 18 (1965), 316.

[17] The London bills of mortality used here are the annual summaries; *A Collection of the Yearly Bills of Mortality, 1657–1758* (London, 1759), and The Company of Parish Clerks of London, *A General Bill of all the Christening and Burials . . . 1764–1803*, British Library folio 1877 e.1. The bills, originally designed to record deaths of the plague in the city of London, began to catalogue other causes of death and included the outparishes beyond the city walls by the mid-seventeenth century.

[18] London infant mortality data reproduced from Edward Shorter, *The Making of the Modern Family* (rev. ed., New York, 1977), 354; Colyton data from E. A. Wrigley, "Mortality in Pre-Industrial England: The Example of Colyton, Devon, Over Three Centuries," *Daedalus* 97 (Spring, 1968), 570–571; North Shropshire data from R. E. Jones, "Infant Mortality in Rural North Shropshire, 1661–1810," *Population Studies* 30 (July, 1976), 314; Nottingham data from J. D. Chambers, "Three Essays on the Population and Economic Change in the Midlands," in *Population in History* (D. V. Glass and D. E. C. Eversley eds., Chicago, 1965), 351.

[19] Edward Shorter, "Maternal Sentiment and Death in Childbirth: A New Agenda for Psychohistory" read to the MSSB Conference on Quantification and Psychohistory, University of Texas, April 1977, 17 and after; David Hunt, *Parents and Children in History, The Psychology of Family Life in Early Modern France* (reprinted New York, 1972), 122. That wet-nursing was a form of delayed infanticide for some mothers in England cannot be denied. It was also the fashion among the best families, who did not wish nor expect their offspring to die from it. It was not so common around London; see Roger A. P. Finlay, "Population and Fertility in London 1580–1650," *Journal of Family History* 4 (Spring, 1979), Table 9, p. 35. The gradual reduction of wet-nursing in the realm nevertheless is an indication of increasing domestic affection; see Shorter, *Making of the Modern Family*, 175–185.

It must be noted that "baptism" is not a totally reliable measure of successful birth, for dissenters, Catholics, and others might be excluded. Another problem with using the death of newborns as an indicator of maternal indifference to children, and hence of the potential for deliberate infanticide, is that the exact age of death is not always given to or obtained by parish officials. See Thomas R. Forbes, "By What Disease or Casuality: The Changing Face of Death in London," *Journal of the History of Medicine and Allied Sciences* 31 (October 1976), 402.

[20] Shorter, "Maternal Sentiment," 31.

[21] Langer, "Infanticide: A Historical Survey," 359–360; Thomas McKeown, *The Modern Rise of Population* 146–147; E. A. Wrigley, *Population and History*, 126.

[22] Price and wage series from R. B. Mitchell and Phyllis Deane, *Abstract of British Historical Statistics* (Cambridge, England, 1962), 346–347, 480, and T. S. Ashton, *Economic Fluctuations in England, 1700–1800* (Oxford, England, 1959), 181. After much thought, we elected not to use actual bread prices as our measure. That figure might be held down by the "assize of bread" when in fact bread was quite scarce.

[23] Maris Vinovskis, "Mortality Rates and Trends in Massachusetts Before 1860," *Journal of Economic History* 32 (1972), 198–199; Philip J. Greven, *Four Generations: Population, Land, and Family in Colonial Andover, Massachusetts* (Ithaca, N.Y., 1970), 189; Susan L. Norton, "Population Growth in Colonial America, A Study of Ipswich, Massachusetts," *Population Studies* 25 (July, 1971), 440–441. On the declining fortunes of the poor in the city of Boston, see Gary B. Nash, "Urban Wealth and Poverty in Pre-Revolutionary America," *The Journal of Interdisciplinary History* 6 (Spring, 1976), 562 and after. For some of the older towns, the crisis reached higher strata of society and was more permanent, see Robert Gross, *The Minutemen and Their World* (New York, 1976), 105–106.

[24] Daniel Scott Smith and Michael Hindus, "Premarital Pregnancy in America, 1640–1971: An Overview and Interpretation," 553; Smith, "Parental Power and Marriage Patterns," *Journal of Marriage and the Family* 35 (August, 1973), 419–428; John F. Walzer, "A Period of Ambivalence: Eighteenth-Century American Childhood," in *The History of Childhood* (Lloyd B. DeMause, ed.), 351–382.

CHAPTER 6

[1] Naomi D. Hunard, *The King's Pardon for Homicide Before A.D. 1307* (Oxford, 1969), 162; *Calendar of the Patent Rolls, Elizabeth I*, 6 v., (London, 1939–1973), I, 36–37, II, 493, 533, III, 192, 234, 434, IV, 75, V, 23, 447, VI, 12. Tyndall's case March 18, 1594 Essex assize, 35/36/1.

[2] Nigel Walker, *Crime and Insanity in England, 1: The Historical Perspective*, 127. On notions of legal insanity before the McNaughton rule, see Charles Palmer Phillips, *The Law Concerning Lunatics, Idiots, & Persons of Unsound Mind* (London, 1858), 45, and William C. J. Meredith, *Insanity as a Criminal Defense* (Montreal, 1931), Chapter 3.

[3] Phillip J. Resnick, "Murder of the Newborn: A Psychiatric Review of Neonaticide," 1414–1420. Resnick's estimate of female responsibility agrees with the statistics presented in earlier chapters of this monograph. For Adcock's case, December 17, 1584, December, 1585 see "Calendar of Essex Quarter Session Records," XII, 136, 197; March 13, 1589 Essex assize, 35/31/1.

[4] Cooper's case, *OBSP*, December 11, 1736; Robinson's case, *OBSP*, October 15, 1718.

[5] Resnick, "Child Murder by Parents: A Psychiatric Review of Filicide," 77–78; Edward S. Stern, "The Medea Complex," *Journal of Mental Science* 94 (1948), 330; Knyght's case, July 3, 1589, Essex assize 35/31/2.

[6] Resnick, "Filicide," 329–332; A. H. Chapman, "Obessions of Infanticide," *Archives of General Psychiatry*, I (1959), 12–16; Thøger Harder, "The Psychopathology of Infanticide," *Acta Psychiatrica Scandianavica* 43 (1967), 179–233.

[7] Godfrey's case, September 25, 1584 *Middlesex County Records, I, Indictments* (Jeffreason ed.,) 54, Heyden's case, September 16, 1705; "Calendar of Essex Assize Files," Hindes' case, *OBSP*, May, 1768; Smith's case in Norman L. Faberow, "Cultural History of Suicide," in *Suicide in Different Cultures* (Faberow ed., Baltimore, 1975, 10.

[8] Kellum, "English Infanticide," 379; Ivy Pinchbeck and Margaret Hewitt, *Children in English Society I* (London, 1969), 15; *Children and Youth in America, A Documentary History* (Robert Bremmer, ed.), I, 123–124.

[9] Selwyn M. Smith, *The Battered Child Syndrome* (London, 1975), 61–74; Brandt F. Steele and Carl B. Pollack, "A Psychiatric Study of Parents Who Abuse Infants and Small Children," in *The Battered Child* (Ray E. Helfer and C. Henry Kempe eds., Chicago, 1968), 103–146; David C. Gil, "Incidence of Child Abuse and Demographic Characteristics of Persons Involved . . ." in *The Battered Child* (Helfer and Kempe, eds.), 19–49.

[10] Joseph C. Rheingold, *The Fear of Being a Woman* (New York, 1964), 143.

[11] Archer's case, March 15, 1613, Essex assize 35/55/1; Inghram's case, July 25, 1625, Essex assize 35/67/1.

[12] Yonge's case, April 19, 1588 "Middlesex Gaol Delivery Rolls," Greater London record office, Smyth's case, March 29, 1560 Essex assize, 35/2/3 and *Calendar Patent Rolls, Elizabeth I,* III, 234, Capell's case, December 12, 1614; Le Hardy, ed., *Middlesex Sessions,* II, Joan Renvoize, *Children in Danger* (London, 1975), 66.

[13] The difficulty of determining the nonaccidental character of children's injuries is discussed in Thomas McHenry, et al., "Unsuspected Trauma with Multiple Skeletal Injuries During Infancy and Childhood," in *The Battered Child* [1974] (Jerome E. Leavitt, ed.), 12–17.

[14] Morris' case, *OBSP*, September 7, 1772; Robert Malcolmson, "Infanticide in the 18th Century," in *Crime in England* (Cockburn, ed.), 205—206.

[15] On the law of abortion, Peter C. Hoffer and N. E. H. Hull, "Abortion in English and American Law to 1803" read to the American Society for Legal History Conference, Chicago, October 21, 1978.

[16] Lyveston's Case, May 27, 1611 "Middlesex Gaol Delivery Calendar, 1607–1612," 113; Robinson's case, February 22–24, 1616, *Middlesex Sessions* (Le Hardy, ed.), III, 175, 189.

[17] Penekemes' case, November 23, 1609 "Middlesex Gaol Delivery Calendar," 134; see also *Middlesex Sessions* (Le Hardy, ed.), I, 262–263, 428, 438.

[18] Oath reproduced from Thomas R. Forbes, *The Midwife and the Witch* (New Haven, 1966), 145. Only New York and Massachusetts required oaths in the colonies; Jane B. Donegan, "Midwifery in America: 1760–1860" (Ph.D. diss. Syracuse University), 1972, 9–10. The canon law connection between infanticide and abortion is discussed in Eugene Quay, "Justifiable Abortion— Medical and Legal Foundations, Part II," *The Georgetown Law Journal* 49 (Spring, 1961), 395–538.

[19] W. Walter Meninger Jr., "The Roots of Urban Crime, A Psychodynamic Perspective," in *Crime in Urban Society* (Barbara N. McLennan ed., New York, 1970), 3–22; Howard Jones, *Crime in a Changing Society* (Baltimore, 1965), 24–25; on the eighteenth-century London "criminal class," see *Nineteenth Century Crime in England* (J. J. Tobias ed., New York, 1965), 22–50.

EPILOGUE

[1] Edward Lankster, "Infanticide in London," *The British Medical Journal* (January 17, 1863), 77; William B. Ryan, *Infanticide: Its Law, Prevalence, Prevention and History* (London, 1862), 58–67; Dyer's case is in Jonathan Goodman, *Bloody Versicles, The Rhymes of Crime* (Newton-Abbott, England, 1971), 100. On the Infant Life Preservation Act of 1872, see Sister Mary Clemens DeHaan, "The Case of Margaret Waters and the Infant Life Protection Act of 1872" (M.A. diss., University of Notre Dame), 1965.

[2] State of South Carolina v. Elizabeth Green, 4 Strobhart 128 (1836), cited in Jack K. Williams, *Vogues in Villany, Crime & Retribution in Ante-bellum South Carolina* (Columbia, S.C., 1959), 22; Todd L. Savitt, "Smothering and Overlaying of Virginia Slave Children: A Suggested Explanation," *Bulletin of the History of Medicine* 3 (1975), 400–404; Sherman's case is in Richard D. Wolff, *Famous Old New England Murders* (Brattleboro, Vt., 1942), 52–91; infanticide law citations appear in Thomas J. Michie, *A Treatise on the Law of Homicide,* II (Charlottesville, Va., 1914), 1124–1124.

[3] *Miami* [Fla.] *Herald.* July 23, 1978, *Columbus* [Ohio] *Dispatch,* November 5, 1976 November 11, 1976; *New York Post,* December 4, 1976, *Chicago Tribune,* April 26, 1978.

[4] *Crime in the United States, Uniform Crime Reporters, 1961–1976* (Washington, D.C., 1962–1977), table 18, on "Murder by Circumstances," one of whose categories is "Parent Killing Child." The British data is from Evelyn Gibson and S. Klein, *Murder 1957 to 1968, A Home Office Statistical Division Report on Murder in England and Wales* (London, 1969).

[5] *Kenny's Outlines of Criminal Law* (19th ed., J. W. C. Turner ed., Cambridge, England, 1966), 195–197.

Index

Table of Statutes